SIDELIGHT:
BIBLE CHARACTERS

Being Extracts From Sermons

Preached By

J.C.PHILPOT

Edited By

G.D.Buss

2002

Gospel Standard Trust Publications
12(b) Roundwood Lane
Harpenden
Herts
AL5 3DD
England

ISBN 1 897837 34 7

First printed in this format : 2002

Printed by:
Olive Press Limited
73 The Green, Stotfold
Hitchin
Hertfordshire
SG5 4AN

PREFACE

The name of J. C. Philpot will need no recommendation to many into whose hands this little volume may fall. His sermons and writings have refreshed the living Church of Christ, long after he entered into the rest which remaineth for the people of God. Truly, his works do follow him.

One of the features of the published sermons of J. C. Philpot, is the manner in which he introduced the subject. Believing, very forcibly, that Scripture should always be taken in the context in which the Holy Spirit placed it, the opening comments often were expositions in their own right. It was this commendable feature of J. C. Philpot's sermons which gave rise to this little volume, which is made up of extracts from the opening remarks of his sermons, particularly as they throw light on some of the Bible characters— some prominent, others less known—which the Holy Spirit has left in the Word, as a record for us to profit by.

Writing to Mr. Godwin in March 1848, J. C. Philpot says: "O, my friend, what is all preaching, or all the gifts in the world, unless the power of God accompany it to the soul!"

Thus may it please the Lord to accompany these spiritual fragments with divine power, even as the five loaves and two fishes were multiplied in the hands of the Redeemer, in feeding the multitude.

G. D. Buss
May 2002

CONTENTS

INTRODUCTION[1]

THE TYPES IN SCRIPTURE

We find in the Old Testament not only what are usually called types, that is, representative things, but typical persons, that is, representative characters. Let me explain my meaning a little more clearly and distinctly. And first, what is the exact meaning of the word "type"? The word "type" signifies, literally, a blow, and thence the effect of a blow—a mark or impression made by it. Thus we find Thomas, speaking after the resurrection: "Except I shall see in His hands the print of the nails." The word "print" is, in the original, "type"; that is, the impression made by the nails driven into the hands of Christ upon the cross. If you were walking by the seaside and pressed your foot down into the damp sand, the impression left by it would be a type or mark of your foot, as well as of the force whereby you brought it down upon the sand. The Queen's head upon the coin of the realm, is a type or representation of the head of the Queen, and is so as being the effect of a blow or other force impressed upon the die. Similarly, the metal letters, used in printing, are called types, as being representations of certain forms derived from what is termed the matrix, that is, the mould or cavity in which the letter is formed, and which gives it its peculiar shape. You will excuse these simple explanations, as they may serve to give you a clearer and fuller idea of what is meant by the word "type" when applied to spiritual things. A type, then, in this sense, means a representation of an object, and, as found in the Old Testament, a prophetic representation of a New Testament object, which is usually called the anti-type, because it corresponds to, and is the fulfillment of, the original type. The Old Testament is full of these types or prophetic representations of New Testament objects. Thus the paschal lamb was a type of Christ as the Lamb of God. The Tabernacle set up in the wilderness, was a type of the human nature of our Lord Jesus Christ, in which the fulness of the Godhead dwelt, bodily. The brazen serpent was a type of Jesus bearing our sins on the cross. The scapegoat, over which the sins of the people of Israel were confessed and laid, was a type of Christ, as having our sins put upon His head, and bearing them away to a land of forgetfulness. In fact, all the various rites and ceremonies of the Levitical law, together with the sacrifices which were offered up, were all types of the Lord Jesus Christ, and of the blessings and benefits derived from His sufferings, blood shedding and death.

But besides these typical representations of the Lord Jesus Christ in His various covenant characters and relationships, there were also typical persons, as distinct from typical things, who represented Him in a shadowy outline, and yet sufficiently plain and clear enough to draw forth the faith of the Old Testament believers upon the Son of God, who was to be manifested in due time. Thus Joseph was a typical person, and as such, typical of Christ; the chief difference between a typical thing or type, in the strict sense of the word, and a typical person, being this, that the former is more marked, distinct, and clear than the latter. In a type, every part, or well nigh every part, has its significance, as you would see by carefully reading and spiritually understanding the solemn transactions on the great day of atonement.

But you could not say that every part of Joseph's or of David's life was typical and representative. It is quite sufficient that the main outlines should correspond with the anti-type, and not every particular. Thus, that Joseph was sold by his brethren for the price of a servant, that, though cruelly treated by them, he still loved them, that he delivered them from famine, made himself known to them, bore with all their ingratitude, fed and nourished them–in these various points, Joseph resembled and typified Jesus. But we cannot take every event of Joseph's life and say that it was a typical representation which found its fulfillment in the Lord Jesus. So with David, who was eminently a typical representative of the Lord Jesus But, who could take all the events of David's life and make out of them a typical representation of what Christ was in the flesh? In a similar way, and with similar limitations, Aaron was a type of Christ as the great High Priest, over the house of God. Moses, as the mediator of the law on Mount Sinai, was a type of Christ as the Mediator between God and man. Jonah was a type of Christ in being three days and three nights in the belly of the whale. But I need not take up time and attention with dwelling upon these typical personages, as it is a point sufficiently clear.

But I shall now draw your observation to another point—that, in the Old Testament, we find also what I may call, representative characters. The typical persons of whom I have just spoken, typified the Lord Jesus Christ in dim and shadowy outline, but those whom I call representative characters do not so much typify Christ, as they represent the characters of men under various phases. Abraham, for instance, is the representative character of a believer; for those who are blest with faith are said to walk in the steps of faithful Abraham; and as being called "the father of all them that believe," (See Romans 4. 11) whether Jew or Gentile, he is made a pattern, or representative of all who believe with that same faith which was bestowed upon him. Job is a representative character, as eminent for patience, and therefore James says: "Ye have heard of the patience of Job." Similarly, Elijah was a representative character of a man whose prayers reached the ears of God, and who, so to speak, shut and opened the windows of heaven at will. James, therefore, quotes him as an example of how "the effectual fervent prayer of a righteous man availeth much." In the book of the Prophet Ezekiel, God mentions the names of three men—Noah, Daniel, and Job—as being eminent for righteousness; they may, therefore, be viewed as representative characters of righteous men.

But we have also in that wonderful Book, the Word of the living God, representative characters of things. Thus Ahithophel, a double faced hypocrite, who could go to the house of God in company with David, and then sell him into the hands of his worst foe, may be viewed as a representative of hypocrisy. Doeg, as a representative of a man of blood, who would shrink from no crime, and fall upon the priests of the Lord, when the servants of Saul would not put forth their hand against them. So Nabal is a representative of a drunken, covetous churl, whom wealth has hardened, and drunkenness besotted, till he is ripe for the sword of slaughter. Similarly, Jonathan may be accepted as a representative of warm, affectionate, brotherly love; and his father, Saul, as an awful instance of gifts without grace, and that a man may be an instrument in the hands of God to accomplish His purposes, but lives and dies in his sins.

But to what do all these observations tend? To this point—to show that there are those people in the Word of God who are representative characters; and that as Abraham represented a believer, Job, one eminent for patience, and Jeremiah, a prophet who wept over the calamities of Israel; so others, such as Moab may also represent a character which is to be found in the Church of God and which will be my main object to unfold to your view that with God's blessing, you may gather up instruction, encouragement, or if need be, warning, reproof, and admonition from it.

Israel, in ancient days,
Not only had a view
Of Sinai in a blaze,
But learned the gospel too;
The types and figures were a glass
In which they saw the Saviour's face.

The paschal sacrifice,
The blood besprinkled door,
Seen with enlightened eyes,
And once applied with power,
Would teach the need of other blood
To reconcile the soul to God.

The lamb, the dove, set forth
His perfect innocence,
Whose blood of matchless worth,
Should be the soul's defence;
For He who can for sin atone,
Must have no failings of His own.

The scapegoat on his head
The people's trespass bore,
And to the desert led
Was to be seen no more:
In him our Surety seemed to say,
"Behold, I bear your sins away."

Dipped in his fellow's blood,
The living, bird went free;
The type, well understood,
Expressed the sinner's plea,
Described a guilty soul enlarged,
And by a Saviour's death discharged.

Jesus, I love to trace
Throughout the sacred page
The footsteps of Thy grace,
The same in every age.
O grant that I may faithful be
To clearer light vouchsafed to me!

JACOB[2]

"I will not let Thee go except Thou bless me." Genesis 32. 26.

The person by whom, and the circumstances under which these words were uttered, must be familiar to all here who have a tolerable acquaintance with the letter of God's written Word. I need therefore scarcely remark that they are the words of Jacob when he was wrestling with the angel. He was returning to his native land under peculiar circumstances. Though he was a child of God, his treachery against his brother, Esau, had not passed unnoticed and unchastised by the Lord. Nay, for that very reason, because he was a child, he experienced chastisement. And not only so, but he had the very same treachery that he had shown to his brother, Esau, amply repaid into his own bosom, by the Lord's permitting Laban to deceive him in a point where his tenderest affections were concerned, besides oppressing and defrauding him continually.

After a lapse, then, of twenty years, at the Lord's command he escapes from the hard oppression of Laban, and sets out to return to the land of his fathers and to his kindred. (See Genesis 31. 3). But, after being miraculously delivered from the vengeance of Laban, and drawing near the borders of Canaan, he learns to his dismay that his brother, Esau, was at hand with four hundred men. The recollection of his former treachery flashing upon his conscience, immediately filled him with the deepest distress and alarm, lest his justly incensed brother should fall upon him, all defenceless as he was, and "smite the mother with the children."

But what was Jacob's resource? He did what every child of God must do under similar circumstances. He goes and wrestles with the Lord. We read that he "was left alone." He allowed no person to be present while he poured out his soul before God. Thus Hezekiah "turned his face toward the wall," when the sentence of death was felt in his conscience. (See Isaiah 38. 2). Thus Nehemiah stood in silence behind the king, when he put up a secret petition on Jerusalem's behalf. (See Nehemiah 2. 4). Thus Moses lay at the feet of the Lord on the shore of the Red Sea, venting the secret groaning of his soul, unknown and unnoticed by the ear of man. Thus Hannah, too, left her husband and her rival, to pour out her soul before the Lord in solitude and sorrow. (See 1 Samuel 1. 9, 10, 15). And thus, in the days of His flesh, the Man of Sorrows "went out into a mountain to pray, and continued all night in prayer to God" (Luke 6. 12); and again, deserted and alone in the gloomy garden of Gethsemane, "offered up prayers and supplications with strong crying and tears unto Him that was able to save Him from death, and was heard in that He feared." (Hebrews 5. 7). Sweet and encouraging examples for living souls to follow!

But O how graciously did God interpose on Jacob's behalf! When reduced to extremity, the Lord showed Himself. And how did He appear? In human shape; not indeed by an actual assumption of real flesh and blood, as some have vainly imagined; *that* was reserved for the time when He took part of the flesh and blood of the children. (See Hebrews 2. 14). The Son of God could only once become actually incarnate; and therefore, these appearances in the Old Testament of the Lord in human shape, were but shadowy representations, and preached to the Church, that then was, the future incarnation of the Son of God. With this "Man," as He is called in the Word, Jacob wrestled till the break of day; and whilst thus wrestling, these words, the words of the text, burst forth, in the extremity of Jacobs case, from his lips: "I will not let Thee go, except Thou bless me."

> Fear thou not, distressed believer;
> Venture on His mighty name;
> He is able to deliver,
> And His love is still the same.
> Can His pity or his power
> Suffer thee to pray in vain?
> Wait but His appointed hour,
> And thy suit thou shalt obtain.

JOSEPH[3]

—

"Joseph is a fruitful bough." Genesis 49. 22.

—

In reading the Old Testament records, we are struck with this circumstance, that, in the case of many of those who were raised up for signal purposes in the Church of God, there was that in their birth or in their life, which was marked by some peculiar divine interposition. One feature of this nature is particularly remarkable in some of the most eminent saints and servants of God—that their mothers were naturally sterile. It was so, you know, with the mother of Isaac, the heir of promise; of Jacob; of Samson; of Samuel, in a very marked instance. It was so (to come to New Testament times) with the mother of John the Baptist. The mothers of all these eminent servants of God were naturally barren; and, as a desire for offspring amounted, in Eastern wives, almost to a passion, God seems to have taken occasion thereby to manifest His prerogative, and display the sovereignty of His power, even in the circumstances of their natural birth. You find this in the case of Joseph, also. As he was to be a marked instrument in the hands of God, eminent as a saint, and eminent as a preserver of God's people in Egypt, he had to spring, in the same way, from a barren mother. You well know that Rachel was sterile, and that, in answer to prayer, God gave her a son, whom she named "Joseph," as a pledge (the name signifying, "He shall add") of further offspring.

Now Jacob, before he dies, assembles his sons around him, and pronounces over them, what we cannot exactly call blessings, because to some, no blessing was given—but be bids them gather themselves together that he may tell them that which shall befall them in the last days. Having spoken of one, and then another, he comes down, at last, to Joseph; and upon him he pronounces this special benediction, "Joseph," says he, "is a fruitful bough, even a fruitful bough by a well; whose branches run over the wall. The archers have sorely grieved him, and shot at him, and hated him: But his bow abode in strength, and the arms of his hands were made strong by the hands of the mighty God of Jacob."

MOSES[4]

"... Moses verily was faithful in all his house as a servant ..."
Hebrews 3. 5.

Moses, the man of God, in being appointed to lead the children of Israel out of Egypt, had the heaviest load put upon his shoulders that mortal back could bear, and, at the same time, the highest honour given into his charge that human hands could receive. It was not a task that he took upon himself, unchosen, uncalled, uncommissioned. It was no flight of heroism that impelled, no outburst of patriotic ardour that urged him on to liberate his countrymen from slavery; but the express call and commission of God. It may indeed be said of him, as is said, by the apostle, of Aaron, his brother—"no man taketh this honour unto himself, but he that is called of God," (Hebrews 5. 4). Nor was it a matter of chance or good fortune—that infidel way of putting God out of the government of His own world—that such a man as Moses was found just at the very time when he was specially needed. It was not more of chance that Moses led the children of Israel out of Egypt, than it was of chance that Jacob, four hundred and thirty years before, went down to sojourn there, or of chance that at the end of the four hundred and thirty years, to the very day, they came up with a mighty hand and a stretched out arm. (See Exodus 12. 41). God, who sees the end from the beginning, chose him for the work, and every step that He took with him was to qualify him for it.

If we view these steps with a spiritual eye, we shall see wisdom and power stamped upon them all. By a special interposition of God's providential eye and hand, Moses was preserved from a watery grave by the daughter of the very king who had determined on the extirpation of his race; by her, was brought up in the court of his greatest foe; and became so enriched in her affections as not only to be made her adopted son, but, as her heir, at Pharaoh's death, would have ascended the throne of Egypt. He was instructed in all the learning of the Egyptians, and had at his command all the luxuries that wealth could purchase, and all the honours that a prince and heir apparent at a royal court could receive. Yet, amidst all the blandishments of that luxurious life—in the full splendour of that regal

12

city, the very ruins of which now fill travellers with astonishment and admiration—grace touched his heart, and taught him to esteem, "the reproach of Christ greater riches than the treasures in Egypt." Grace opened his eyes to see that God had a people here below, that the outcast Israel, the despised slaves who were building the treasure cities, and whose hands were soiled with mud and clay, were the chosen of the Almighty; and, cleaving to them in faith and affection, he preferred "rather to suffer affliction with the people of God, than to enjoy the pleasures of sin for a season."

Thus, when Moses came to years, he "refused to be called the son of Pharaoh's daughter;" renounced all the honours and enjoyments of an earthly court, and went forth to visit his brethren. I need not mention the cause of his being obliged to leave Egypt and flee to the land of Midian, where he tarried forty years. And O what lessons he learnt there!—lessons without which he would have been utterly unqualified to lead the children of Israel out of Egypt. Many a stripling, hot from the university, or fresh from the academy, thinks himself fully qualified to lead the Church of God. But Moses was not qualified, when full forty years old, by all the learning of Egypt, to lead the children of Israel. He had to go for forty years into the wilderness, not merely to learn by painful experience the external hardships to be met with there, but the temptations and trials, the perils and sufferings of a wilderness heart, where there are fiery serpents that bite more venomously, and angry scorpions that sting more sharply than any serpent or any scorpion that drags its slimy trail across the barren sand. There he learnt the terrors of God in that law of which he was afterwards the typical Mediator, and there he learnt, too, the blessings of the gospel, when he saw, by the eye of faith, an incarnate God in the burning bush, and became "the friend of God" by the manifestation of everlasting love to his soul.

Time will not permit me to enter further into the character of Moses. We find him, in the Book of Deuteronomy, at the end of the forty years sojourn in the wilderness, matured, not only in years, like as a shock of corn cometh in its season, but ripened also in grace. Under the special inspiration and influence of the Holy Ghost, causing His doctrine to drop as the rain, and His speech to distil as the dew, he poured forth his soul in that sweet language which animates every chapter and almost every word of this blessed book — what we may call this Old Testament gospel, the Book of Deuteronomy. If blessed with any measure of his faith, what a view we shall have, in our text, of the special privileges and rich favours that belong to the Church of God!

For us, then, so far as we belong to the spiritual Israel, Moses stood upon Pisgah's top, and viewed the land spread before his eyes; for us he looked down upon the tents of Israel spread at his feet, and, inspired of the Holy Ghost, to view in Israel after the flesh, Israel after the Spirit, he saw, by faith, the mystical body of Jesus—the Bride of the Lamb—the Church of the first-born, whose names are written in heaven. Viewing, then, by faith, the privileges and mercies vouchsafed to the Church of God, he burst forth in the words of our text:—"Happy art thou, O Israel: who is like unto thee, O people saved by the LORD, the Shield of thy help, and who is the Sword of thy excellency! and thine enemies shall be found liars unto thee; and thou shalt tread upon their high places."

Happy are they to whom the Lord
His gracious name makes known!
And by his Spirit and his word
Adopts them for his own.

He calls them to a mercy-seat,
And hears their humble prayer,
And when within his house they meet,
They find his presence near.

The force of their united cries
No power can long withstand;
For Jesus helps them from the skies,
By his almighty hand.

Then mountains sink at once to plains,
And light from darkness springs;
Each seeming loss improves their gains;
Each trouble comfort brings.

Dear Lord, assist our souls to pay
The debt of praise we owe;
That we enjoy a gospel-day,
And heaven begun below.

THE HIGH PRIEST[5]

"A merciful and faithful High Priest in things pertaining to God, ..." Hebrews 2. 17.

The grand object of the Epistle to the Hebrews is to set forth the high priesthood of the Lord Jesus Christ. Into that subject we cannot now fully enter; and yet our text leads us (and may the Lord lead us by the text) into some attempt to shew who this High Priest is, of whom the apostle here speaks. And I think the simplest, and therefore the best division of the subject will be, to shew, as the Lord may enable, in the *first* place, the mind of the Spirit in the 15th verse, "We have not a High Priest which cannot be touched with the feeling of our infirmities; but was in all points tempted like as we are, yet without sin:" and *secondly, the exhortation* which flows from, and is based upon the priesthood of Immanuel, "Let us therefore come boldly unto the throne of grace, that we may obtain mercy, and find grace to help in time of need."

1. I need scarcely take up your time by shewing at any length in what way the high priest under the law was a type and figure of the Lord Jesus Christ. And yet, there are certain points of resemblance, and certain points of difference, which it will be desirable to enter into, in order to illustrate and set forth more clearly the mind and meaning of the Holy Ghost in the words before us.

There were three points of *resemblance* (there were more, but I confine myself to three) between the high priest under the law and the great "High Priest over the house of God." The first was, that the high priest offered sacrifices; the second, that he made intercession for the sins of the people on the great day of atonement, by taking incense beaten small, and, putting it on the coals which were taken off the brazen altar, with it entered into the most holy place (see Leviticus 16.12, 13); and the third, that he blessed the people (see Numbers 6. 23).

Now, in these three points did the high priest under the law beautifully resemble and set forth the great "High Priest over the house of God." But O, how feeble the resemblance! how dim the type! how shadowy the figure! The high priest under the law could only offer the blood of bulls and goats, which can never take away sin; the great "High Priest over the house of God" offered Himself— His own body and His own soul—that precious, precious blood, which "cleanseth from all sin." The high priest under the law could only offer incense upon the coals taken from off the brazen altar; the great "High Priest over the house of God" is offering daily the virtue of His sacrifice by "making intercession for us." The high priest under the law could only pronounce the blessing in so many words; he could not *give* or communicate that blessing to the soul; the great "High Priest over the house of God" can and does bless the soul with the sweet manifestations of his lovingkindness and tender mercy.

But again. There are points of *difference,* as well as points of resemblance.

1. The high priest under the law was but a man; the great "High Priest over the house of God" is God-man, "Immanuel, God with us," the eternal "Son of the Father, in Truth and love," having taken our nature into union with His own divine and glorious Person.

2. The high priest under the law died in course of years, and was succeeded by a high priest as mortal as himself (see Hebrews 7. 23); but the great High Priest above liveth for evermore to "make intercession for us."

3. The high priest under the law might be (and the apostle seems to make some allusion to the circumstance here) one who had no sympathy nor fellow feeling for the infirmities and sins of those for whom he made sacrifice; he might be like some of our priestly Dons who seem all holiness, and have no tender heart to feel compassion for backsliders, and those that are out of the way: but the great "High Priest over the house of God," the apostle here says, is one that is "touched with the feeling of our infirmities."

4. The high priest under the law might be, or might not be, tempted; he might be, or he might not be, a man who knew the plague of his own heart and the workings of his fallen nature, and therefore might not be "tempted in all points" like unto those for whom he might sacrifice; but the great "High Priest over the house of God" was "tempted in all points like as we are," and therefore can

have, and does have a fellow feeling for the tempted.[*]

5. The high priest under the law was a sinner; but the great "High Priest over the house of God" is spotless, without sin, "holy, harmless, undefiled, separate from sinners, and made higher than the heavens."

> With joy we meditate the grace
> Of our High Priest above;
> His heart is made of tenderness;
> His bowels melt with love.
>
> Touched with a sympathy within,
> He knows our feeble frame;
> He knows what sore temptations mean,
> For He has felt the same.
>
> But spotless, innocent, and pure,
> The great Redeemer stood,
> While Satan's fiery darts He bore,
> And did resist to blood.
>
> He, in the days of feeble flesh,
> Poured out His cries and tears;
> And, in His measure, feels afresh
> What every member bears.
>
> He'll never quench the smoking flax,
> But raise it to a flame;
> The bruisèd reed He never breaks,
> Nor scorns the meanest name.
>
> Then let our humble faith address
> His mercy and His power;
> We shall obtain delivering grace,
> In the distressing hour.

---

[*] Philpot does not infer here that Christ had a fallen nature with which He was tempted. Rather he makes the point of His sympathy with His tempted people, being assailed Himself by the Evil One who nevertheless found nothing in Him. *Ed*

THE CHILDREN OF ISRAEL[6]

"… they came to Marah, …" Exodus 15. 23

The children of Israel after the flesh, were a typical people; and therefore, the dealings of God with them were typical and figurative of His dealings with the spiritual Israel. When we see this, and read the Old Testament Scriptures with an enlightened eye, what beauty does it add to the sacred page! We read these records then, not as so many historical documents, but as descriptive of the children of God, and of His mercy, love and grace towards them. And thus their experience becomes brought home to our own heart and our own bosom. We can see in them, our own features, and read in the dealings of God with them, the dealings of God with our own souls now.

I need not run through the history of the children of Israel to prove this. Every step they took is, more or less, a proof that the Lord dealt with them outwardly, as He deals with His spiritual Israel inwardly. Their state, for instance, in Egypt, typified the death and darkness of the people of God before they are quickened by the blessed Spirit. The paschal lamb of which they partook, and the blood sprinkled upon the lintel and doorposts, showed forth the redemption of Christ, and the application of His precious blood to the conscience. The passing through the Red Sea signifies the baptism wherewith they are baptized, when the love of God is shed abroad in their hearts by the Holy Ghost; and their seeing their enemies dead upon the seashore, signifies the rejoicing of a child of God at finding his sins cast into the sea, and overthrown into dead carcasses by the mighty power of Christ.

But we come now to a strange passage in their history. They little expected, as we should little expect, that so heavy a trial would come immediately upon the back of this astonishing deliverance. And what was this trial? "They went three days in the wilderness, and found no water." In this humid climate, we can scarcely conceive what a privation this must have been. But we should not like, even in this wet clime, to be without water for three days. No water to drink, no water to wash with! But look at this vast multitude, amounting to two million, wandering in a barren desert, with a scorching sun above, and parched sands beneath; men, women, children, and cattle, languishing, and all but for dying of thirst! And this for three days! One can scarcely conceive what a privation; what a scene of horror it must have been. But, at the end of three days, water is discovered. They catch a glimpse of palm trees in the wilderness, and perhaps see the glimmering of streams beneath them. You may well conceive what joy would fill the camp. We may well imagine what a universal shout of exultation there would be. What hurrying on to partake of the waters that glistened before their eye in the distance! But alas! when they came there, a further disappointment awaited them. "They came to Marah, and they could not drink of the waters of Marah." Though for three days they had been without water, and were dying from thirst, yet, when they came to these waters, they were so bitter and brackish that absolutely they could not drink! What a blow! What a stroke upon stroke! This was, indeed, striking the dying dead. This was, indeed, adding grief to their sorrow, and heaping calamity upon calamity.

Well, what did they do? What you and I, no doubt, would have done. They murmured and rebelled, and cried out against Moses for bringing them out of Egypt, with it's beautiful Nile, and leading them into this wilderness, where, for three days, they had no water; and when they came to water, it was so bitter they could not drink. And what did Moses do? Did he join with them? Did he encourage their murmuring, or take part in their rebellion? No. He did what he ever did, and what every child of God must sooner or later do—he "cried unto the LORD." And did he cry in vain? Was the Lord a "God afar off, and not at hand"? Was His hand shortened, that it could not save, or His ear heavy, that it could not hear? No. The same almighty arm that had brought them through the Red Sea, found a way of escape. "The LORD shewed him a tree, which when he had cast into the waters, the waters were made sweet."

HANNAH[7]

"He raiseth up the poor out of the dust …" 1 Samuel 2. 8.

Most of you are probably familiar, not only with the name of the person who uttered these words, but also with the circumstances under which they were spoken by her. But lest any should not immediately recollect the passage, I will just observe that they are the words of Hannah, the mother of the prophet, Samuel, and that the circumstances under which they were spoken, were when she brought her infant son, and presented him before the Lord, that he might be His for ever. Her heart, it appears, was then so enlarged, and her soul so comforted and strengthened by beholding her infant son as the manifested answer to her prayers, that she burst forth into that song of thanksgiving of which the text forms a portion.

It may be desirable, with God's blessing, to trace out a few leading particulars of Hannah's case.

I believe, that, in Scripture, there are typical characters, as well as what are more properly called "types", or typical things; and Hannah appears to me to have been one of these typical characters. By typical characters, in this sense, I mean, not in the same way as Aaron, or Solomon, were types of Christ, but certain persons whose history and experience are typical, or representative, of God's dealings with His people, or of characters that should arise in the Church. The history of Hannah affords us more than one instance of these typical characters. We read, for instance, (see 1 Samuel 1. 1, 2) that Elkanah "had two wives; the name of the one was Hannah, and the name of the other Peninnah; and Peninnah had children, but Hannah had no children." Elkanah seems to me to typify the Lord Jesus — I think we may fairly assume this, without doing violence to the figure; and his two wives seem to represent the Church, Peninnah the *professing*, and Hannah the *possessing* Church.[*] Let us see if the figure will bear us out in this interpretation. Peninnah, in type, represents the professing Church. As having a form of godliness, and a name to live, she had a vast superiority outwardly over her rival, for

---

[*] In making this analogy, Philpot does not infer that the merely professing church is ever married to Christ but only appears to be so. *Ed.*

20

she was fruitful, whilst Hannah was barren. This points out the superiority, in outward fruit, which many professors have over God's spiritually-taught children. But, we may observe that, in Peninnah's fruitfulness there was nothing manifested of a supernatural character. She had children in the common course of nature, as other married women have them; there was nothing peculiarly providential, nothing eminently striking, nothing miraculous; but all took place in the usual course.

Now, this strikingly represents the way in which mere professors of religion bring forth their good works. The fruits they produce are not wrought in them by miracle; they do not spring out of a supernatural operation upon their consciences; but they are brought forth, from time to time, in the mere course of nature, without any galling disappointment on account of previous barrenness, without any earnest cry that the Lord would work powerfully in their soul, without any manifested answer to the prayer that He would make them fruitful in every good word and work. But these good works and religious performances, on which they pride themselves so highly, are brought forth by them in the usual course of nature, by the mere exertion of the creature, utterly independent of any work of the Holy Ghost upon their heart.

But this fruitfulness of Peninnah much galled and pained her barren rival, as the zeal, devotedness, piety and amiability, evident in many professors, often exceedingly gall the children of God. For they are spiritually, what Hannah was naturally—barren. Thus they cannot bring forth good works in the usual process of nature. Barrenness, impotency, and helplessness, have so completely paralysed them, that they require a supernatural, and I might say, without going too far, a miraculous, operation of the Holy Ghost upon their conscience, just as Hannah required, to speak with all delicacy, a miraculous operation upon her womb to bring forth fruit. They are, then, exceedingly pained and galled by seeing how fruitful mere professors of religion are, whilst they continue barren and fruitless. Thus fruitful Peninnahs can pray, whilst barren Hannahs cannot put up a single breath of spiritual prayer: the one can always believe, whilst the other cannot raise up a single grain of living faith in their heart; the former can hope, whilst the latter, at times, are ready to sink down well nigh into despair: the dead can be happy, while the living are often overwhelmed in misery; the carnal can read the Bible, chapter after chapter, while the spiritual can scarcely open it, at times, on account of the temptations which assail them; and the graceless can walk in the path of religion with all the ease and comfort in the world, whilst the gracious, like Asaph, are plagued all the day long, and chastened every morning. As Peninnah, too, taunted her rival with her own fruitfulness and her barrenness, so the mere professors of religion often taunt God's people with their want of good works, compared with their own superior and abundant religious performances. They sneer at those who profess spiritual religion as backward, where they are forward. They therefore upbraid them, as Peninnah did Hannah, for their barrenness, and charge them with religious indifference, or, what they call, their Antinomian slothfulness; and, with an inward satisfaction and wonderful self-complacency, compare their own abundant fruitfulness with their barrenness.

But what was the effect of these taunts, or, rather, what was the effect of the secret pangs produced in Hannah's soul by the sense of her barrenness? It was that she turned away from everything, and went with her burden to the Lord. And there is one thing which I would not wish to omit, which is, that even her husband himself could not comfort her. Elkanah, indeed, said to her: "Am not I better to thee than ten sons?" Applying the type: Is not the Lord Jesus better to the souls of His people than all the good works in the world, or even than all the testimonies He might give them? Is not the Giver better than the gift? The Husband better than the wedding ring? Aye, indeed, He is; but then, for want of the gift, they often doubt their interest in the Giver, and the ring being missing, their title to the Bridegroom is called in question. Living souls cannot be satisfied with the bare knowledge that Christ is a Husband to His Church, when they come short of a feeling testimony and a blessed witness, in their own consciences, that He is so to them. We cannot, indeed, fully carry the figure out, for Christ can comfort His people with a word, whilst Elkanah, with all his attempts, and even double portion of gifts and love, could not comfort his wife, because she was lacking in that one point on which she had so set her heart. But what was her resort and refuge? She went where every child of God will go—to the Lord, and she went to Him in soul-trouble, as every child of God will sooner or later do.

It is not feeble prayers, customary prayers, what I may call regular prayers, that draw forth the Lord's manifested compassion, and bring down an answer of mercy and peace; but it is when the Spirit intercedes in the soul, with groanings which cannot be uttered; when it walks in the steps of its great Covenant Head, of whom we read, that "being in an agony He prayed more earnestly." (Luke 22. 44). When the soul cries unto the Lord in the depth of soul trouble; it is *then* that the most High God bows down His ear and answers. Was it not so with Hannah? No sooner had she, poured out her soul before the Lord, and spoken to Him out of the abundance of her complaint and grief, than, though Eli at first mistook her case, the Lord spoke a word by his lips to her soul, which wiped away the tears from her eyes, and sent her home in peace. And when her prayer was manifestly granted, and she came up with the answer in her arms, her infant son, Samuel, which means, "heard of God," when she held him up before the LORD as the answer to her prayer; her soul was melted into thanksgiving, the voice of praise burst forth from her lips, and the Holy Ghost has recorded her song of triumph for our comfort and instruction.

In themselves as weak as worms,
How can poor believers stand,
When temptations, foes, and storms,
Press them close on every hand?

Weak, indeed, they feel they are,
But they know the Throne of Grace;
And the God who answers prayer,
Helps them when they seek His face.

Though the Lord awhile delay,
Succour they at length obtain;
He who taught their hearts to pray,
Will not let them cry in vain.

Wrestling prayer can wonders do;
Bring relief in deepest straits!
Prayer can force a passage through
Iron bars and brazen gates.

For the wonders He has wrought,
Let us now our praises give;
And, by sweet experience taught,
Call upon Him while we live.

THE PSALMIST DAVID[8]

—

"… the sweet psalmist of Israel …" 2 Samuel 24. 23

—

The Psalms are a blessed manual of Christian experience, and well may I call them so; for I think I may confidently say, that there is not a single spiritual feeling in the bosom of a child of God which is not expressed, with greater or less distinctness, in that inspired record of the hidden life of the saints of old. By way of proof, take a few examples. If, for instance, guilt lies hard and heavy upon your conscience, if sins press you down as an intolerable load, where can you find your feelings so clearly and so beautifully expressed as in Psalms 38, 40, 51, 69? In these, and other Psalms of a similar kind —"penitential," as they are sometimes called—you almost seem to hear the sighs, cries, groans, and prayers of a soul bleeding, as it were, under a sense of the wrath of God, and imploring forgiveness. You could never have framed such petitions, or made such confessions, as the Holy Ghost has there put into the heart and mouth of David; yet you find that the feelings expressed in those petitions and confessions are the very experience of your breast. But, take another view of this heavenly manual of all true vital experience. Say that the Lord, in the depth of His infinite mercy, in the exceeding riches of His abounding grace, is pleased to break your iron chains, to turn your captivity, and to bless you with a sense of His pardoning love, where can you find the joyous feelings of a liberated soul more blessedly expressed than in Psalms 32, 103, and 116? where the sweet psalmist of Israel, like Naphtali, "a hind let loose," praises and blesses God for loosing his bonds, for redeeming his life from destruction, and crowning him with lovingkindness and tender mercies. Or if, after a sense of mercy received, you are called upon to walk in temptation's fiery path, where can you find your temptations to despond or rebel, to murmur and fret at your own trials, and to envy the ease and prosperity of others, more clearly expressed than in Psalms 37 and 73? If you are walking in darkness and have no bright shining light, where can you find the feelings of your soul more vividly and pathetically described than in Psalm 88? —the experience of Heman. If you carry about with you a deep and

24

daily sense of God's heart-searching presence, feeling that every thought of your bosom lies naked and open before the eyes of Him with whom you have to do, where can you find such a description of God's omnipresence and omniscience as in Psalm 139? If you desire to make the Word of God your daily study, that your heart and life should be conformed thereunto; or if you are, from time to time, breathing forth your desires that it may be opened up to your understanding, and applied with power to your soul, where can you find your spiritual feelings so beautifully expressed as in Psalm 119? So I might run through the whole experience of a Christian—what I may call the spiritual gamut of his soul, from the lowest bass to the highest treble, and point out that there is not a single note or half-tone of divine teaching and gracious feeling, which may not be set down and sounded on this harp of many strings. Yes, I may say, from the babe in grace, to the father in Christ; from the first cry for mercy in the soul of the convinced sinner, to the last hallelujah of the expiring saint; God has written the whole experience of His children, as with a ray of light, in this blessed manual of spiritual pains and pleasures, sighs and songs, prayers and praises, groans from the gates of hell, and shoutings at the portals of heaven.

Now, with His gracious help, see and admire God's wisdom in this. You might have various feelings in your soul, either of sorrow or joy, and yet be much tried in your mind whether they were spiritual feelings—whether, for instance, your convictions were the workings of mere natural conscience, and your joys the sparks from a fire of your own kindling, or whether they were each the inwrought work of God. But when you see God's own stamp that He has fixed upon certain feelings or certain experiences, and that, by putting them into His Book, He has, Himself, given His attestation that they are such as He approves of, you have an evidence that what you feel of sorrow or joy, has been wrought in you by the power of God. You might otherwise rise into fanaticism and enthusiasm through false joys, or sink into despair through false fears, mistaking, in each case, the workings of nature for the workings of grace. But this being the Manual, the guide, the test, the proof, it keeps the child of God, on the one hand, from setting up the enthusiastic feelings of nature as marks of grace, and, on the other, from sinking into despondency, as fearing that his experience is not wrought in his soul by a divine operation. O, how good it would be for us, to make the Psalms more our bosom companion! Not merely as persons sometimes carry their Bibles in their bosom, as was the habit of a gentleman whom I knew in Ireland, whose life was preserved thereby, the slugs from the assassin's gun, aimed at his breast, being thus intercepted; but to carry in the inmost heart this Manual of Christian experience, and find it daily unfolding more and more its beauty and blessedness to our admiring souls.

But there is one feature in the Psalms to which I wish now more particularly to call your attention, as it is connected much with our text. In other parts of Scripture, God speaks to man; in the Psalms, man speaks to God; and as he speaks to Him as one brought near by the power of His grace, there is a holy familiarity, a blessed drawing near, a sweet pouring forth of heart and spirit into the bosom of God, which we find rarely paralleled in any other part of Scripture. As Enoch, of old, walked with God in sacred fellowship and divine intimacy, so there is in the Psalms a blessed familiarity unfolded to our view, whereby David, and other holy men of God, walked before Him in the light of His countenance.

O bless the Lord, my soul!
Let all within me join,
And aid my tongue to bless His name,
Whose favours are divine.

O bless the Lord, my soul!
Nor let His mercies lie
Forgotten in unthankfulness,
And without praises die.

'Tis He forgives thy sins;
'Tis He relieves thy pain;
'Tis He that heals thy sicknesses,
And makes thee young again.

He crowns thy life with love,
When ransomed from the grave;
He that redeemed my soul from hell
Has sovereign power to save.

He fills the poor with good;
He gives the sufferers rest;
The Lord has judgments for the proud,
And justice for the oppressed.

His wondrous works and ways
He made by Moses known;
But sent the world His truth and grace,
By His beloved Son.

SOLOMON[9]

"Vanity of vanities, saith the Preacher, vanity of vanities; all is vanity." Ecclesiastes 1. 2.

What an instance is King Solomon of the vanity of all creature enjoyments, and the emptiness of all creature attainments! The wisest of mankind, and yet often doing actions of which a fool might be ashamed! Speaking, by divine inspiration, in The Proverbs, the language of most blessed instruction, and yet, in conduct, violating well nigh every precept which he had given, and acting in direct opposition to every proverb which he had inculcated! Seated in peace upon the throne of his father, David, enjoying every pleasure which wealth could minister, supplied with every gratification that his senses could delight in, and then forced, in his old age, to write "vanity and vexation of spirit" upon them all! In his declining years, reaping the bitter fruits of backsliding from God, and giving to us in this book of Ecclesiastes, (which appears to be the expression of his repentance), his own dearly-bought experience of the utter vanity and instability of all creature enjoyments and expectations, and brought to see that there was nothing worth having, but the fear of the Lord in the heart in blessed exercise, and the testimony of God in the soul!

Now, in this diversified experience through which King Solomon passed, he learned lessons which were not to be arrived at through any other channel. It was not in vain that he had every gratification presented to his carnal mind; it was not in vain that he made himself "gardens and orchards," and gat him "men singers and women singers," that whatsoever his "eyes desired" "he kept not from them," and "withheld not" his "heart from any joy;" for he "looked on all the works that" his "hands had wrought, and on the labour that" he "had laboured to do: and, behold, all was vanity and vexation of spirit, and there was no profit under the sun" (see Ecclesiastes 2. 5, 8, 10, 11). He has thus set up a beacon that we might, with God's blessing, avoid the shoals on which he struck; a lighthouse blazes forth, that we might not fall foul on the sands on which his frail bark too often ran; and thus, the Spirit of God sealing the instruction upon our souls, that we might steer clear of those reefs which the Holy Ghost has traced out by his pen in this chart of his perilous navigation.

Let no one misunderstand me. I believe that Solomon was a gracious character, and that he is now in glory; but the Lord left him to do many things which showed plainly that he was but a man, and which clearly prove that he was not able to act up to the lessons of divine wisdom which he taught. And, he is a striking instance how that, placed as he was in an eminent situation, and not being kept by the grace of God from the many temptations to which his very wealth and station exposed him, he was carried away by them, to the future distress of his soul. But, in this chequered path of experience, he learned a lesson, the fruit of which is recorded in this chapter, that "the times" and "the seasons, ... the Father hath put in His own power." (See Acts 1. 7).

Solomon's experience gave the freewill that lurked in his bosom a fatal stab, turned upside down the wisdom of the creature, broke into a thousand shivers all his fleshly righteousness, and convinced him deeply of the sovereignty of God reigning over all his purposes, words, and works. And therefore, as the fruit of this wisdom, which was communicated through the channel of personal experience, he came to this solemn conclusion, that "to every thing there is a season, and a time to every purpose under the heaven:" that these times are in the hands of God; not to be precipitated, not to be retarded; not depending upon the movements of the creature; not fluctuating with the restless tide of human will and purpose, but fixed in the sovereign decrees of Jehovah, and fulfilled at such a moment and in such a manner as it pleaseth Him "who worketh all things after the counsel of His own will:" (Ephesians 1. 11).

How vain are all things here below;
How false, and yet how fair!
Each pleasure has its poison too,
And every sweet a snare.

Our dearest joys, and dearest friends,
The partners of our blood,
How they divide our wavering minds,
And leave but half for God!

Dear Saviour, let Thy beauties be
My soul's eternal food;
And grace command my heart away
From all created good.

LEMUEL[10]

—

"Open thy mouth for the dumb." Proverbs 31. 8.

—

There is, I believe, some difference of opinion as to who this King Lemuel was, to whom the words I have just read were addressed, by his mother, together with the remaining portion of the chapter; but the best-founded opinion seems to be, that he was King Solomon, and that he is here called, Lemuel, either because it was an endearing appellation wherewith his mother was used to address him—a kind of fondling term, instead of Solomon, or else that it was a name of Solomon, in addition to that whereby he is generally known. For, it was the practice amongst the Hebrews to give various names to the same individual. So Jehoiachin is called, in Jeremiah, Coniah (see Jeremiah 22. 24), and in the same way, Solomon himself is, in another part of Scripture, called Jedidiah (see 2 Samuel 12. 25); and, therefore, there is reason to believe, that Lemuel here, is merely another name for King Solomon.

The meaning of the word Lemuel is, literally, "unto God", that is, devoted unto God, belonging to God, as the apostle expresses himself, when he speaks of Christ, in one short word, "God's"; "all are yours; And ye are Christ's; and Christ is God's" (1 Corinthians 3. 22, 23), that is, belonging to God. His mother then addresses to her son, King Lemuel, that excellent advice which is contained in the last chapter of the book of Proverbs; and, no doubt, the advice which she laid before him admitted a *literal*, as well as a spiritual, interpretation. There appear to be two errors which men fall into; one is, setting aside the spiritual meaning of a passage altogether, and adopting the literal, and the other is, setting aside the literal altogether, and adopting only the spiritual. There seems little doubt, that, in Scripture there is a literal interpretation, as well as a spiritual one, and that there always is an analogy—a resemblance between the two interpretations; the spiritual interpretation being based upon the literal, and the literal standing as a foundation, on which the spiritual interpretation rests.

Therefore, in endeavouring to trace out the experimental interpretation of these words, which I shall endeavour to lay before you, I mean not to set aside that literal meaning which, doubtless, the words were intended to convey. The mother of Lemuel exhorted him strictly and literally, when, as a king he sat in judgment, to "open" his "mouth for the dumb in the cause of all such as are appointed to destruction." She inculcated upon him, as the judge of his people, as one that sat in the gates of the city to administer justice—that he should open his mouth, "judge righteously, and plead the cause of the poor and needy." But, when we look at the spiritual and ex-perimental meaning of the words, we see that "a greater than Solomon is here", and that Lemuel points at a greater king than ever Solomon was, in all his glory. The word signifies, as I hinted before, devoted unto God—"God's", in a word. Who can be, then, more emphatically pointed at than the Lord of life and glory, who is God's Son and God's servant—God's ambassador, who was devoted to Him, and who was consecrated to Him during His pilgrimage here below, and yet is one with Him in essence, and one with Him in glory?

But it may be asked, if Lemuel here signifies the Lord Jesus Christ, whom can we understand by "His mother", and who is she that she should give Him any advice? How is this to be explained consistently with the analogy of faith, and the Scriptures of truth? What read we in Song of Solomon 3. 11? "Go forth, O ye daughters of Zion, and behold king Solomon with the crown wherewith *His mother* crowned him in the day of His espousals, and in the day of the gladness of His heart." There we have a strictly parallel passage, where King Solomon, who doubtless is Jesus (for the whole book of Canticles is taken up with a description of the loves of Jesus and His Church), is spoken of as having a mother, and being crowned by her. His mother, then, must represent the Church, seeing that the Lord Jesus Christ derived His human nature from a woman, was "made of a woman", as the Scripture speaks, and thus the Church may be said, in this sense, to be the mother of Christ. We have, then, in the text, certain advice which was given to King Lemuel by his mother; and her counsel to him was: "Open thy mouth for the dumb in the cause of all such as are appointed to destruction. Open thy mouth, judge righteously, and plead the cause of the poor and needy."

JEREMIAH (1)[11]

—

"...thou shalt be as My mouth;" Jeremiah 15. 19.

—

Of all the prophets in the Old Testament none, seem to have walked in such a rough and rugged path, respecting the ministry, as Jeremiah. Four distinct circumstances met in his case, which made the prophetical office peculiarly burdensome to him. One was, *the distresses of the times.* The Lord, at that time, was bringing judgments, such as sword, pestilence, and famine, upon the house of Judah; and these judgments falling upon the people of God, as well as upon the ungodly, made Jeremiah's lot peculiarly hard. A *second* circumstance was, *the persecutions that he had to endure,* because he would not prophesy smooth things, and speak peace where there was no peace. A *third* was, that he was left to *know* and *manifest more of the rebellion and peevishness of his depraved nature* than any of the prophets, if perhaps we except Jonah. And a *fourth* was, that *the Lord hid His face from him,* and did not appear for his comfort and deliverance in the way that Jeremiah earnestly longed to enjoy.

These four circumstances, meeting in Jeremiah's case, made his path, as the prophet of the Lord, so rough and rugged. We find him, therefore, in this chapter giving vent to the passionate rebellion of his heart. He says: "Woe is me, my mother, that thou hast borne me a man of strife and a man of contention to the whole earth!" He pities his mother, that ever she gave birth to a child so deeply wading in the waters of strife and contention, and obliged to stand up so boldly in the Lord's name. "I have neither lent on usury, nor men have lent to me on usury; yet every one of them doth curse me." He felt it was a painful path, to endure almost universal odium, when he knew, in his conscience, that he did not deserve it—that he was not one of those wretched usurers who deservedly met with public scorn and hatred, but a friend to Judah and Jerusalem. He therefore pours out his soul to the Lord in these peevish and fretful complaints.

Now, the Lord meets the prophet on these points. He says: "Shall iron break the northern iron and the steel?" that is: Shall this iron hearted oppression that thou art passing under—shall this iron yoke thou art wearing—shall the bows of iron bent against thee—

31

shall the gates of iron closed before thee—in a word, shall this trouble from without and within, which is to thee as hard and as strong as iron, be stronger than the northern iron and the steel of My covenant purposes, eternal counsels, and immutable decrees? Shall the stronger fall before the weaker? The northern iron being so much stronger and better tempered must break the ordinary metal; and the sharp steel must cut it utterly asunder.

This word from the Lord affords the prophet some little comfort; and therefore he answers: "O LORD, Thou knowest: remember me, and visit me, and revenge me of my persecutors; take me not away in Thy long-suffering: know that for Thy sake I have suffered rebuke. Thy words were found, and I did eat them; and Thy word was unto me the joy and rejoicing of mine heart: for I am called by Thy name, O LORD God of Hosts. I sat not in the assembly of the mockers, nor rejoiced; I sat alone because of Thy hand: for Thou hast filled me with indignation. Why is my pain perpetual, and my wound incurable, which refuseth to be healed?" And then, in a most inexcusable burst of passion, he says: "wilt Thou be altogether unto me as a liar?" (What rash, unbecoming words for a creature of the earth, a worm of the dust, to address to the Almighty!) "and as waters that fail?" Hast Thou promised, and wilt Thou not perform? Hast Thou declared Thou wilt appear in my extremity, and shall it not come to pass? Are Thy promises like a deceitful brook, dried up by the summer's sun? (see Job 6. 15). In answer to this passionate cry, passing over with infinite forbearance and long-suffering his unbecoming appeal, the Lord gives him this word to support his fainting spirit: "If thou return, then will I bring thee again, and thou shalt stand before Me: and if thou take forth the precious from the vile, thou shalt be as My mouth."

It is as though the Lord said: If thou return from this passionate, rebellious murmuring, from this unbelief and despondency, and yield thyself up into My hands, then will I bring thee again before this people as My honoured prophet, and thou shalt stand before Me with acceptance as My ministering servant. And is not this thy highest honour—is not this thy greatest privilege—to be as My mouth? Dost thou want more? Have not I chosen thee for this purpose? Have I not called thee—have I not strengthened thee for the work? Is not *that* sufficient? Will I not stand by thee? Will I not bring thee safe through? Will I not honour My own word by thy lips? And canst thou think, when so honoured as to be My mouth to My people, that I will ever leave thee? Thus the Lord supports his fainting spirit, and encourages the prophet still to stand up boldly and faithfully in His name, whether men will hear, or whether they will forbear.

Every servant of the Lord has to endure a measure of what Jeremiah went through. He has to endure persecutions, temptations, assaults from Satan, the workings of a rebellious heart, the hidings of the Lord's countenance, and a whole train of trying circumstances. But, these very things fit him for the ministry, and without them he would be but a dry breast to the Lord's quickened family.

JEREMIAH (2)[12]

—

"… take forth the precious from the vile …" Jeremiah 15. 19.

—

Of all the prophets of the Old Testament, Jeremiah appears to have undergone the largest amount, as well as greatest variety, of suffering for his Lord's sake. Many circumstances concurred to produce this. First, his lot was cast *in a time of great general suffering*. The Lord was pouring out His wrath upon the people of Judah and the inhabitants of Jerusalem. His sore judgments, long denounced, were now being executed. Sword, pestilence and famine were stalking through the land; and, as these were national judgments, the righteous and the unrighteous, the true prophet and the lying priest, the king on the throne and the captive in the dungeon, alike partook of them.

But he had not only a large measure of personal, individual suffering, but, as deeply *sympathising* with a captive people, a besieged city, and a fallen Church, and as identifying himself with the afflictions of Zion, as an eye-witness of the fearful scenes of desolation that were daily spread before his eyes, for these things he wept; his eye ran down with water, because the Comforter that should relieve his soul was far from him: and his children were desolate, because the enemy prevailed. (See Lamentations 1. 16).

Another ingredient in the cup much, also, embittered his lot—*the persecution* and opposition that he met with, in the discharge of his prophetical office. The false prophets of those days always prophesied good and not evil; and thus, by their lies and deceptions, buoyed up the people in a vain security. Their language to the people—and this they pretended they spoke by the inspiration of God—was: "Ye shall not see the sword, neither shall ye have famine; but I will give you assured peace in this place." (See Jeremiah 14. 13). Thus they prophesied lies in the Lord's name, telling the people, even when surrounded by the invading armies of Nebuchadnezzar, that they should not go down to Babylon; that there was to be no captivity of the nation, no destruction of their city, or desolation of their temple; crying out continually: "The temple of the LORD, The temple of the LORD, The temple of the LORD, are these." (See Jeremiah 7. 4). As if, because they were the Lord's people in external covenant, He would never punish them for their sins.

And is not this the exact feature of the false prophets of our day, who will not allow that the people of God ever undergo chastisement for their sins and backslidings? who cry: "Peace, peace," when there is no peace? who neither preach nor practise the precepts of the gospel, but wrap all their ministry up in a system of dry doctrine, and thus deceive the people in the Lord's name, by pretending to be His servants, when He has neither taught nor sent them? As Jeremiah, then, was raised up of the Lord for a special purpose, and "set ... over the nations and over the kingdoms, to root out, and to pull down, and to destroy, and to throw down," as well as "to build, and to plant," (Jeremiah 1. 10), he could not but speak all that the Lord put into his mouth. His tidings, therefore, were heavy tidings, for he had to declare to them that they were to go into captivity, even unto Babylon; that their city was to be taken; their temple to be burnt with fire; and the whole land to be made utterly desolate. This unwelcome news, therefore, stirred up the enmity of the princes, the priests, and the whole people of the land, who had all been propped up by the false prophets, to whom they looked as the mouth of God, to believe themselves sure of His protecting hand.

But, in addition to these outward troubles, Jeremiah appears to have possessed, naturally, a *very rebellious spirit*, which, as stirred up by opposition and persecution, often made him very fretful and unbelieving; and this evil appears, at times, to have gained great power and prevalence over him, for, under its sad influence, he was even sometimes permitted to use, toward the Lord, most unbecoming language, as, for instance, in the words immediately preceding our text: "Why is my pain perpetual, and my wound incurable, which refuseth to be healed? wilt Thou be altogether unto me as a liar, and as waters that fail?" What rebellious, inconsistent, unbecoming language is this! With the exceptions of Job and Jonah, there is scarcely any saint of God, through the whole Scripture, who fell into such rebellious language against the Majesty of heaven. But, no doubt, this rebellious spirit and murmuring tongue, falling back upon him in guilt and shame, produced a large additional measure of grief and trouble.

But, in addition to this, he had to endure great depths of *personal affliction*. He was committed into the court of the prison and had for his subsistence, but a piece of bread daily, given him until all the bread in the city was spent. Thence he was cast into the dungeon full of mud and mire; where he was like to die of hunger, for there was no more bread in the city (see Jeremiah 37. 21; 38. 6, 9).

And when we add to this, that the *light of God's countenance* was often *withdrawn* from him, as a chastisement for his rebellion, we may well see that all this complication of circumstances, filled his soul with trouble, and his mind with confusion. If rebellion against the Lord could be ever excusable, it was in the prophet Jeremiah; for, we may be well sure that nothing but such a weight of sorrow could have drawn from him the passionate words that I have quoted: "Why is my pain perpetual," etc.

But, how does the Lord answer this complaint? What is the solace which He gives to His mourning prophet? What is the balm of consolation which He pours into his bleeding wounds? Not what we should expect, and yet, seen in the light of the Spirit, a relief most blessedly adapted to all the circumstances of his case: "If thou take forth the precious from the vile, thou shalt be as My mouth." It is as if the Lord said: "Jeremiah, My own prophet, whom I have commissioned to bear My tidings to the nations; thou whom I expressly called by My Spirit and grace to this office, that thou shouldest be as My mouth, did I not set thee over the nations and over the kingdoms to root out and to pull down, and to destroy and to throw down every plant and every tree not of My setting, and every building not of My rearing? Why art thou thus filled with rebellion and self-pity at witnessing the effects of thine own work, which I gave thee to do? Why art thou weeping over the miseries of the people whom I am justly punishing? Why, as a soldier of the truth, art thou shrinking from the field of battle, the thunder of the captains, and the shouting? Or why fearest thou persecution from the enemies of God? Know this, for thy comfort and encouragement, that thy highest office and greatest privilege is to be My mouth. Dream not of worldly comfort; think not of a false and unrighteous peace with the ungodly, or of freedom from their persecution, as if, by some compromise, you might disarm their enmity, or win their favour. Banish the thought of such carnal ease, and be satisfied with this one most blessed privilege, that thou art *My mouth*; that I do thee the honour to speak in thee and by thee; that, whatsoever thy sufferings are, or shall be, thou still art My faithful servant; that I will still support thee, hold thee up, and bless thee, and make it manifest to thee, and to all around thee, that I have sent thee, and that My words in thy mouth shall be fulfilled, so that not one jot or tittle of them shall fail." This word from the Lord, as it dropped into the prophet's soul, calmed, no doubt, his rebellious spirit, and brought him to feel, if not to say: "Well, Lord, if I am to be Thy mouth, I can bear all that Thou mayest be pleased to lay upon me. As Thy son and servant, as Thy prophet and minister, let me speak Thy words, not my own. I want not the smiles of men, I only want Thy support, Thy power, and Thy presence, my God, my Father, and my Friend." Such, I believe, is the spirit, and such the feeling of all who are sent to do Jeremiah's work, and through whose lips the God of Jeremiah speaks.

"Seekest great things for thyself? Seek them not." Jeremiah 45. 5.

These words were spoken by Jeremiah, the prophet, to Baruch, the son of Neriah; and they were addressed to him under particular circumstances. It was at the time when the Lord was accomplishing His purpose of carrying His people, Judah, into captivity; when, according to His righteous judgments, the Levitical sacrifices were, for a time, to cease, the temple to be destroyed, and the people to be uprooted from their own city and country, and taken into the land of Babylon. These were times, doubtless, of great temporal affliction. The presence of the invading army must have carried with it all those desolations which that terrible scourge of God invariably brings; and the righteous as well as the wicked must have, alike, suffered in this general calamity. Sword, pestilence, and famine came alike upon all, upon him that swore, as upon him that feared an oath (see Ecclesiastes 9. 2).

But, in the case of the "remnant according to the election of grace," there were superadded to the weight of their temporal calamities the heavy burdens of spiritual affliction. The severe judgments of God upon the land were so many visible testimonies of His displeasure. And it seems as if the experience of God's people in that day was of a character similar to the general gloom. The dark lowering cloud that hung over Jerusalem, cast its shadow over the souls of the living family.

We thus see a connection between Jeremiah's experience in the Lamentations, and the temporal afflictions of Judah; and the same cause may account for the lamentation that Baruch poured out in the words preceding the text, and of which the Lord takes this special notice: "Thus saith the LORD, the God of Israel, unto thee, O Baruch: Thou didst say, Woe is me now! for the LORD hath added grief to my sorrow; I fainted in my sighing, and I find no rest."

Grief added to sorrow—spiritual trials added to temporal trials, soul affliction following upon natural affliction, wave calling to wave, and burden heaped upon burden; and both together so depressing his spirits, so weighing him down, that he fainted in his sighing, and could find no rest.

The Lord doubtless saw in Baruch's heart that which Baruch did not see himself; He saw, lurking there, a secret craving after things which God has never promised to bestow upon His people. He discerned, through the thick veil spread over his heart, that there were immoderate desires working in his bosom, and that he was aiming at things quite inconsistent with the purposes of God, the character of the times, and what was really profitable for his own soul. Viewing, then, with His heart-searching eye what was thus secretly going on in the chambers of imagery, the Lord addressed Himself to the very circumstances of the case: "And seekest thou *great things* for thyself? seek them not: for, behold, I will bring evil upon all flesh, saith the LORD: but thy life will I give unto thee for a prey in all places whither thou goest."

There seems to have been, in Baruch's mind, a secret hope that the Lord would not bring down upon Judah the judgments denounced; at any rate, he appears to have cherished a lurking expectation that he himself would not be involved in them. Amidst all his grief and sorrow, his fainting and sighing, *ambition* was not dead within; and there was a restless aiming at things inconsistent with the afflictions to fall upon his country, and with his own character as a prophet of the Lord. Now, who of us can plead: "Not guilty!", to a similar charge?

My brethren, why these anxious fears,
These warm pursuits and eager cares
For earth and all its gilded toys?
If the whole world you could possess,
It might enchant; it could not bless;
False hopes, vain pleasures, and light joys.

Jesus has said (who surely knew
Much better what we ought to do
Than we can e'er pretend to see),
"No thought e'en for the morrow take;"
And "He that will not for My sake
Relinquish all, 's unworthy Me."

Great things we are not here to crave;
But if we food and raiment have,
Should learn to be therewith content.
Into the world we nothing brought,
Nor can we from it carry aught;
Then walk the way your Master went.

38

CYRUS[14]

—

"I will go before thee, and make the crooked places straight."
Isaiah 45. 2.

—

To whom were these words spoken? To Cyrus. And who was Cyrus? King of Persia. But how came Cyrus to be introduced into the Word of God; and how did it happen that the Lord gave such promises to a heathen monarch? Cyrus, though a heathen prince, was an instrument chosen of God to do an appointed work, which was to overthrow the great Chaldean empire, take the city of Babylon, and restore the children of Israel to their own land; and therefore, one hundred and seventy years before he executed the office thus assigned to him, he was expressly pointed out, and personally addressed by name in the record of inspired prophecy. What a proof is this of the inspiration of God's Word, and that all events are under His appointment and control!

Not only, however, was he thus called by name, but the very work which he had to do was expressly declared long before the necessity arose for its being accomplished. The work for which he was raised up and divinely appointed, was to rescue from captivity the two tribes of Judah and Benjamin, which, as a punishment for their sins, were to be carried into captivity to Babylon, where they were to continue for a definite period, the space, namely, of seventy years. To rescue them, then, from this Babylonish captivity, when the seventy years were expired, and to enable them to return, was the work that Cyrus, in the appointment of God, had to perform. This was a very great work for him to execute, a work, so great, that he could not have performed it unless he had been specially aided by God. For he had to take a city whose walls were fifty cubits thick and two hundred feet high, surrounded by a wide ditch full of water, and defended with one hundred gates of brass. The city was also well manned and well provisioned, and altogether so strong and powerful as to defy every mode of attack then known. If the Lord, therefore, in the words of the text, had not "gone before him;" if He had not broken "in pieces the gates of brass, and cut in sunder the bars of iron:", Cyrus could never have taken that mighty city, but must have been utterly defeated in the attempt.

This, then, is the literal meaning of the text. But does it not admit of a more extensive application? The promise, it is true, was given to Cyrus, and we know was literally fulfilled; but are the words applicable only to Cyrus? Have we no fortress to take, no city of salvation to win? Do we not need the Lord to go before us, and make our crooked places straight? Have we no gates of brass, no bars of iron, which shut out approach and access, and which we need the Lord to break in pieces and cut in sunder for us? Does the road to heaven lie across a smooth, grassy meadow, over which we may quietly walk in the cool of a summer evening, and leisurely amuse ourselves with gathering the flowers and listening to the warbling of the birds? No child of God ever found the way to heaven a flowery path. It is the wide gate and broad way which leads to perdition. It is the strait gate and narrow way, the uphill road, full of difficulties, trials, temptations, and enemies, which leads to heaven, and issues in eternal life. If, then, we be Zion's pilgrims, heavenward and homeward bound, we shall find the need of such promises, in their spiritual fulfilment, as God here gave to Cyrus.

Now I see, whate'er betide,
All is well if Christ be mine;
He has promised to provide;
May He teach me to resign.

When a sense of sin and thrall
Forced me to the sinner's Friend,
He engaged to manage all,
By the way and to the end.

"Cast," He said, "on me thy care;
'Tis enough that I am nigh;
I will all thy burdens bear;
I will all thy needs supply."

Lord, I would indeed submit;
Gladly yield my all to Thee;
What Thy wisdom sees most fit,
Must be surely best for me.

Only when the way is rough,
And the coward flesh would start,
Let Thy promise and Thy love
Cheer and animate my heart.

THE MINOR PROPHETS[15]

—

"… holy men of God spake as they were moved by the Holy Ghost." 2 Peter 1. 21

—

Of the Old Testament Scriptures, taking of them a general view, I do not know a more difficult part to understand than that which is contained in, what are commonly called, "the minor prophets;" that is, the series of prophecies commencing with Hosea and terminating with Malachi. They are called, as you probably know, the minor prophets, not because of any inferiority in inspiration, in authority, or in subject matter, to the greater prophets—Isaiah, Jeremiah, Ezekiel, and Daniel, but on account of the comparative brevity, or smallness in bulk, of their compositions; rarely extending, except Hosea, Amos, Micah and Zechariah, beyond the compass of three or four chapters.

Now, if these minor prophets are so difficult to understand—at least, I have found them so—there must be some reason for this difficulty. But perhaps you see no difficulty; perhaps you are a thorough master of the whole subject, and have penetrated, with an eagle eye, into the whole series, so as to clearly see both their literal and spiritual meaning. But will you allow me to gauge, by a few questions, the depth of this knowledge? Can you understand Obadiah? What meaning would you affix to such a passage as this? "And the house of Jacob shall be a fire, and the house of Joseph a flame, and the house of Esau for stubble, and they shall kindle in them, and devour them; and there shall not be any remaining of the house of Esau; for the LORD hath spoken it." (See Obadiah 18). Are you fully master of Amos? And can you explain the meaning of this verse? "I saw the Lord standing upon the altar: and He said, Smite the lintel of the door, that the posts may shake: and cut them in the head, all of them; and I will slay the last of them with the sword: he that fleeth of them shall not flee away, and he that escapeth of them shall not be delivered." (See Amos 9. 1). Do you understand the meaning of Nahum, where he says: "Where is the dwelling of the lions, and the feeding place of the young lions, where the lion, even the old lion, walked, and the lions whelp, and none made them afraid? The lion did tear in pieces enough for his whelps, and strangled for his lionesses, and filled his holes with prey, and his dens

41

with ravin." (Nahum 2. 11, 12). And do you think you have sounded all the depths of Joel? "O," you say, "I have not thought about the meaning of such passages as those." Then don't think you understand it until you have considered the subject a little more closely, and sounded some of these hidden depths; for you may depend upon it, that these minor prophets, though we may gather up much of their general meaning, are very difficult to understand in their minuter details, and especially when we desire to invest them with a spiritual interpretation. For this difficulty there seem to be several reasons.

First, we are but imperfectly acquainted with the kingdoms, states, and persons, generally, against whom they were uttered, and the events of the period in which the prophets themselves lived; so that, many things which they wrote, though perfectly intelligible at the time when they were written, are very obscure to us now. Thus Obadiah prophesies of the destruction of Edom, which was a country to the south of Canaan, and chiefly remarkable for its rock-hewn city, situated in a narrow, inaccessible defile, formerly called Selah, but now Petra. The prophet therefore says: "The pride of thine heart hath deceived thee, thou that dwellest in the clefts of the rock, whose habitation is high; that saith in his heart, Who shall bring me down to the ground? Though thou exalt thyself as the eagle, and though thou set thy nest among the stars, thence will I bring thee down, saith the LORD." (See Obadiah 3, 4). But how little is now known of the ancient state of Edom? So Nahum prophesies the destruction of Nineveh. At the time of their prophecies, both of these were flourishing cities, but now, neither of them has an inhabitant; and till, a few years ago the very site of Nineveh was unknown.

Another reason to my mind is, that some of the events which are prophesied are still unfulfilled, as for instance: "And they of the south shall possess the mount of Esau; and they of the plain the Philistines: and they shall possess the fields of Ephraim, and the fields of Samaria: and Benjamin shall possess Gilead." (See Obadiah 19). The full meaning, therefore, of the minor prophets may not be understood until the events to which they refer are accomplished.

There is also a third reason for this difficulty, viz. the harmonising of the literal and spiritual meaning, which cannot well be done whilst the former is obscure.

But the question may perhaps arise in your mind: "If these prophecies are so difficult to understand, why do you preach from them? This morning you took your text out of Hosea, one of the minor prophets; and this evening you are taking your text out of Zephaniah, another of the minor prophets. Are you come this evening with some of these difficulties—to raise up giants that you may kill them, and set us enigmas that you may solve them?" God forbid! I would rather clear up difficulties than make or state them. But you will please to observe that, though there may be great difficulties in fully understanding these minor prophets, yet there are many very blessed passages in them; sweet openings up of experimental truth; most gracious and suitable promises given for the consolation of the Church of God in all ages. We must ever bear in mind this feature in all the prophets, that, as regards the people of God, all their prophecies are promises; and therefore, prophecies being promises, they are all in a state of continual fulfilment. God's dealings with His Church are the same in all ages; for He Himself is "the same yesterday, and to-day, and for ever;" and thus, if many of these prophecies look forward into the dim and distant future, when they will have their full completion, yet there is a continual fulfilment of them as containing, in their bosom, every promised blessing to the saints of God. It is, I may add, this peculiar feature of divine revelation which makes the reading of the Scripture of the Old Testament profitable, and furnishes us, both as ministers and hearers, with food for instruction, consolation, and edification in right-eousness.

Say, Christian, wouldst thou thrive
In knowledge of thy Lord?
Against no Scripture ever strive,
But tremble at His word.

Revere the sacred page;
To injure any part
Betrays, with blind and feeble rage,
A hard and haughty heart.

If aught there dark appear,
Bewail thy want of sight;
No imperfection can be there,
For all God's words are right.

The Scriptures and the Lord
Bear one tremendous name;
The written and the incarnate Word
In all things are the same.

JONAH[16]

—

"Yet will I look again toward Thy holy temple." Jonah 2. 4.

—

It is a great mercy for God's people that the account which the Holy Ghost has given of the saints in the Scriptures, is very different from the opinions which men form of them by nature. If we attend to the conceptions that the human heart naturally forms of saints, we should believe them to be a kind of intermediate being, betwixt us and angels, far removed from all the frailties, sins and imperfections of humanity, never overtaken by slips and falls, but continually walking in the "beauty of holiness".

But God has not recorded such imaginary saints in the Scriptures; and, to beat down these foolish ideas, He has given us an account of the drunkenness of Noah, the incest of Lot, the unbelief of Abraham, the peevishness of Moses, the adultery of David, the idolatry of Solomon, the pride of Hezekiah, the cowardice of Mark, and the cursing and swearing of Peter.

But why has the Holy Ghost left on record these sins and slips of the saints? I believe, chiefly, for three reasons. *First*, that it might teach us that they were saved by grace as poor, lost, and ruined sinners, in the same way as we hope to be saved. *Secondly*, that their slips and falls might be so many beacons and warnings, to guard the people of God against being overtaken by the same sins, as the apostle speaks: "Now all these things happened to them for ensamples: and they are written for our admonition," (see 1 Corinthians 10. 11). And *thirdly*, that the people of God, should they be overtaken by sin, might not be cast into despair; but that, from seeing recorded in the Scriptures the slips and failings of the saints of old, they might be lifted up from their despondency, and brought once more to hope in the Lord.

Of all the recorded prophets, Jonah perhaps stumbles us, naturally, the most. His disobedient, rebellious conduct, before the Lord so signally chastised him; and his impetuous language after he had received such a chastisement, and such a deliverance, when he said: "I do well to be angry, even unto death," have often stumbled those who know neither the depths of the human heart, nor the

44

heights of God's superabounding grace! And yet, I believe, there are many of God's family who have felt comforted and encouraged, not only by Jonah's rebellious conduct, but also by his perverse and unbecoming words. Not that they dare justify the one, nor approve of the other; but those who really know themselves, and have a deep sense of their baseness and abominable vileness before God, are sometimes enabled to derive a little sweetness from seeing to what lengths God's people, who are evidently His saints, and even His inspired prophets, have been permitted to go.

I need hardly, perhaps, remind you, that the words of the text were uttered by Jonah when he was in the whale's belly. It was there he spake them in the bitterness of his soul; it was there that these words of sad despondency, and yet of strong faith, burst from his lips: "Then I said, I am cast out of Thy sight; yet I will look again toward Thy holy temple!"

See a poor sinner, dearest Lord,
Whose soul, encouraged by Thy word,
At mercy's footstool would remain,
And there would look, and look again.

How oft deceived by self and pride,
Has my poor heart been turned aside;
And, Jonah like, has fled from Thee,
Till Thou hast looked again on me!

Ah! bring a wretched wanderer home,
And to Thy footstool let me come,
And tell Thee all my grief and pain,
And wait and look, and look again.

Take courage, then, my trembling soul;
One look from Christ shall make thee whole;
Trust thou in Him; 'tis not in vain;
But wait and look, and look again.

EPHRAIM[17]

—

"Is Ephraim My dear son? Is he a pleasant child? Jeremiah 31. 20.

—

Before I enter into the spiritual meaning of these words, it will be necessary to see the connection of the passage with what precedes it. There is no more fruitful parent of error than to take detached portions of God's Word, separated from their connection. Only so far as light is cast upon the Word of God by the blessed Spirit, and we, in that light, see its spiritual meaning, are we able to arrive at any right understanding of it; but, that meaning will not be one distorted from the connection, nor one wrested from the place that it occupies, as a link torn from a complete chain, but will, for the most part, be in harmony with the context.

The words of the text are the language of Ephraim; but they are the language of Ephraim under particular circumstances, and, as passing through a particular experience. They are not a promise thrown down for anybody to pick up; they are not words to be taken at random into everybody's lips. Nor are they a promise addressed generally to the Church of God; but they set forth an experience of a peculiar nature; and therefore, only so far as we have some acquaintance with that experience, are the words suitable to us.

We will, then, with God's blessing, look back a little at this and the preceding chapter (for they are both closely connected), and endeavour, with God's help, to trace out what was the experience of Ephraim *at the time* that he uttered these words; and then we shall perhaps more clearly see the difference between the language of faith and the language of presumption.

In the twelfth verse of the preceding chapter, the Lord says: "Therefore will I be unto Ephraim as a moth, and to the house of Judah as rottenness." This casts a light on the dealings of God with Ephraim. Ephraim had wrapped himself up in a robe; he had covered himself with a garment, but not of God's Spirit. Now the Lord threatens that He will "be unto Ephraim as a moth." That is, He will fret this garment; He will (to use a familiar expression) make holes in it; it shall not be a complete garment to cover him, but it shall be moth-eaten and rotten, so that, dropping to pieces bit by bit, it could neither cover his nakedness nor shield him from God's all-searching eye. We find the Psalmist, in Psalm 39. 11, making use of the same figure: and a very striking one it is. "When Thou with rebukes dost correct man for iniquity, Thou makest his beauty to consume away like a moth:" or, as it is in the old version, preserved in the Common Prayer Book, "like as it were a moth fretting a garment."

These words, then, show us just where Ephraim was in soul experience. Ephraim does not represent one destitute of spiritual light and life, but a quickened vessel of mercy, and yet one who, for want of the moth and the rottenness, was wrapping himself up in a garment, not of God's giving, nor of the Spirit's application, that is, not the glorious robe of Christ's imputed righteousness cast around him by the Spirit of God.

"How shall I give thee up?"
('Tis Jesus speaks the word)
"I am the sinner's only hope;
I am thy gracious Lord.

"Rebellious thou hast been,
And art rebellious still;
But since in love I took thee in,
My promise I'll fulfil.

"I've bound thee up secure,
'Midst all the rage of hell;
The curse thou never shalt endure,
For I'm unchangeable.

"My son, give Me thy heart;
Let Me thy sorrows bear;
'Tis not thy caution, power, or art,
Can save thee from despair."

Lord, captivate my soul;
Subdue the power of sin;
My vile corruptions, O control;
Let faith the battle win.

ZACHARIAS AND THOMAS[18]

"Be not faithless but believing." John 20. 27.

Unbelief is a damning sin, where it reigns; but not a damning sin, where it exists, and is opposed. In other words, it is the *dominion, not the existence,* of unbelief in the heart, that excludes from the kingdom of heaven. The reprobate are an instance of the *former;* for they live and die under the power of unbelief; as the Lord said: "If ye believe not that I am He, ye shall die in your sins." (See John 8. 24). "He that believeth and is baptized shall be saved; but he that believeth not shall be damned." (See Mark 16. 16). And the quickened elect are an instance of *the latter.*

We can scarcely find recorded two more striking instances of the existence of unbelief in the hearts of God's people, than that of Thomas, and of Zacharias. Yet, the very unbelief of Thomas, in whose heart the spirit of infidelity worked so powerfully that he would not believe that the Lord had risen from the dead, except he should see in His hands the print of the nails, and put his finger into the print of the nails, and thrust his hand into His side, was, doubtless, overruled, not only for the good of the Church in all time, but for the good, also, of the unbelieving disciple, when his infidelity was effectually overcome by the power of the Lord communicating faith to his soul through the words, "be not faithless, but believing." His belief became all the stronger for having been so powerfully assailed.

And so, doubtless, it was with Zacharias, who, as the penalty of his unbelief, was shut up for nine months in mute silence. For, when the Lord loosed his tongue, he "was filled," we read, "with the Holy Ghost, and prophesied," in that blessed hymn of praise which we have recorded, at the end of the first chapter of Luke's Gospel.

The question, then, is not whether we have unbelief in our heart, but whether this unbelief is resisted. If we have nothing there but unbelief, woe be to us! But if this indwelling unbelief is, by a principle of grace, opposed, resisted, and struggled against, the conflict will eventually end in victory.

JOHN THE BAPTIST[19]

—

"And blessed is he, whosoever shall not be offended in Me." Matthew 11. 6.

—

A question has been raised, whether, in sending this message to the Lord Jesus, John the Baptist wished to satisfy his own mind, or the minds of his disciples. Some have thought that John the Baptist could never have entertained any suspicion in his mind whether Jesus was the Messiah. And thus, to vindicate John's honour, they have supposed it was the unbelief of his disciples that John wishes to remove. I do not profess to have a decided opinion upon the matter; but I cannot see why John, considering the circumstances in which he was placed, might not have had suspicions working in his bosom. Was he not a man like ourselves? Did he not carry in his bosom the same unbelieving and infidel heart that we are possessed of? And, considering his circumstances, that he was shut up in prison, that the Lord did not appear to release him, might not a suspicion of this nature have crossed his breast—Am I the forerunner of the Messiah, and will He not come to release me out of this dungeon? I do not see that it impairs the character of John to allow he had these suspicions, these doubtful thoughts in his mind, knowing what unbelieving hearts we all possess.

But, whether it was to satisfy the mind of John, or whether it was to satisfy the minds of John's disciples, the answer of the Lord was: "Go and shew John again those things which ye do hear and see." It appears from a parallel passage, Luke 7. 21, that the Lord wrought several miracles before their eyes: "And in that same hour He cured many of their infirmities and plagues, and of evil spirits; and unto many that were blind He gave sight." Thus, He could appeal to their own senses, and say: "Go and shew John again those things which ye do hear and see."—Does he doubt My mission? Does any suspicion cross his bosom whether I am the Son of God? Tell him what ye have seen, what ye have heard, that these things may support his wavering faith, that they may strengthen his faltering feet. Tell him the miracles which you have seen performed by My hands—"The blind receive their sight, and the lame walk, the lepers are cleansed, and the deaf hear, the dead are raised up, and the poor have the gospel preached to them." And then, as an intimation adapted to the wavering faith of John the Baptist, or of his disciples, He adds: "And blessed is he, whosoever shall not be offended in Me."

Jesus, and shall it ever be,
A mortal man ashamed of Thee?
Ashamed of Thee, whom angels praise;
Whose glories shine to endless days?

Ashamed of Jesus! sooner far
Let evening blush to own a star;
He sheds His beams of light divine
O'er this benighted soul of mine.

Ashamed of Jesus! just as soon
Let midnight be ashamed of noon;
'Tis midnight with my soul till He,
Bright Morning Star, bids darkness flee.

Ashamed of Jesus! that dear Friend,
On whom my hopes of heaven depend!
No; when I blush, be this my shame,
That I no more revere His name.

Ashamed of Jesus! yes, I may,
When I've no guilt to wash away;
No tear to wipe; no good to crave;
No fears to quell; no soul to save.

Till then, nor is my boasting vain,
Till then I boast a Saviour slain;
And O may this my glory be,
That Christ is not ashamed of me.

His institutions would I prize;
Take up my cross, the shame despise;
Dare to defend His noble cause,
And yield obedience to His laws.

MARTHA, MARY AND LAZARUS[20]

—

"Now Jesus loved Martha, and her sister, and Lazarus." John 11. 5.

—

What a beautiful, what an interesting family picture has the Holy Ghost, by the pen of the apostle John, drawn in the sacred narrative of the gracious household which once dwelt in the little village of Bethany, near Jerusalem. In it, we seem to see the rare spectacle of a family living together in happy harmony, united by the strong ties of nature, and united still more closely by the firmer, and more enduring, bonds of grace—Martha, Mary, Lazarus. What an echo there is in our heart to these names. May we not also picture to ourselves our gracious Lord, when He had been at Jerusalem, wearied—for we know He was subject to human infirmity, and could be weary, for He, once, sat weary on Samaria's well—when our gracious Lord returned from Jerusalem, wearied in body and grieved in spirit, how He would come to this happy household, and there solace Himself with the company of these two gracious sisters and their, no less gracious brother, for we read that "Jesus loved Martha, and her sister, and Lazarus." (See John 11. 5).

Our Lord went about doing good, and spent much of His time, and exercised much of His ministry, in Galilee; which, being situated in the north part of the Holy Land, lay at a considerable distance from Bethany. But, it would appear that, at this time, He was not in Galilee, but beyond Jordan, in the place where John at first baptized, which lay at some distance to the east of Jerusalem. Now, when He was thus absent, engaged in performing His gracious errands of mercy, a dark cloud began to gather over this happy household. It might have been, at first, only as small as a man's hand, but it gathered thick and fast, and every hour seemed to hang upon them more and more densely. Lazarus had fallen ill. Now, the first movement of his gracious sisters was to send a message to their dear Lord, that he whom He loved was sick. They knew His power as well as His love; and that as by the one He would at once come, so by the other He could at once heal. They naturally, therefore, expected that He would come speedily in a case so urgent as this, for in that climate disease makes rapid progress, and were doubtless looking out every day and almost every hour for His arrival.

But Lazarus gets worse and worse every hour. Denser, darker are the clouds which hang over the house. Jesus tarries; for we read that "when He had heard therefore that he was sick, He abode two days still in the same place where He was." Jesus comes not. All hope dies in their breast. The disease gradually increases until, at last, Lazarus sinks under its pressure. Now, what a mercy it was for these two sisters, and their brother too, that Jesus did not come; and may I not add, for the Church of God also, for all time? What treasures of mercy and grace were involved in His delay! What a stupendous miracle gave occasion for Him to work! What a demonstration of His power it afforded; that He was, truly, the Son of God! And what a lasting blessing has it been made to successive generations of saints! Though the Lord well knew, in His omniscient mind, all that was transpiring in that little household, yet, for His own wise and gracious purpose, His footsteps tarried, and mercy made Him stay for a while, as mercy made Him come at last.

I need not dwell further upon the features of this interesting narrative, though every part of it is pregnant with holy instruction, but shall come, at once, to that part which engages our attention. It is the interview of Martha with the Lord, at Bethany. Martha, true to her character, could not stay at home; she was a restless body, for, on a later occasion when she had obtained the Lord's company, she could not be satisfied with merely listening to His gracious conversation. She must needs think about the dinner, nay, come and ask Him to bid her sister help her to set it out properly, and not spend her time so—I will not say unnecessarily—but, so long sitting at the feet of Jesus. Like many of our Martha's, she loved religion and the things of God; but, being a bustling, active character, worldly business would intrude on her mind, and to this she would sometimes give a first place, when it ought to have had but the second. Are you not sometimes like her, thinking more of business than of Christ, and even in the house of prayer, instead of listening to the word, are thinking about the dinner?

Martha, then, true to her character, leaves Mary at home, praying, watching and waiting upon God in secret, and hurries out at the very first tidings of His arrival; but, as soon as she meets Him, almost in the language of reproach, not very unlike the way in which she addressed the Redeemer with respect to her sister upon another occasion, says: "Lord, if Thou hadst been here, my brother had not died." Do not the words sound almost as if she was reproaching the Lord because He was not there? And yet, the blessed woman, with all her infirmities, had faith in her soul, and this faith manifested itself in the midst of her complaint. "But I know, that even now,"— though the case seems so desperate—"I know, that even now, whatsoever Thou wilt ask of God, God will give it Thee." O, Martha, thy faith was somewhat lacking here! Thou shouldest have looked a little higher than this, and seen that He was the true God Himself who stood before thee, and that He had but to speak the word, and Lazarus would rise. Thou shouldest have seen that He held creation in His fists, and that life and death were at His supreme disposal. Jesus, in that calm, blessed manner in which our Lord ever spoke, unruffled, unmoved, in all the quiet dignity and glorious majesty of Godhead, saith unto her: "Thy brother shall rise again." Martha still shows faith, and yet, evidently, mixed with much weakness. "Martha saith unto Him, I know that he shall rise again in the resurrection at the last day." Then the Lord uttered those words which I shall, with God's help and blessing, endeavour to lay open, and bring before you this afternoon: "Jesus said unto her, I am the Resurrection, and the Life: he that believeth in Me, though he were dead, yet shall he live: And whosoever liveth and believeth in Me shall never die. Believest thou this?"

The love of Christ is rich and free;
Fixed on His own eternally;
Nor earth, nor hell, can it remove;
Long as He lives, His own He'll love.

His loving heart engaged to be
Their everlasting Surety;
'Twas love that took their cause in hand,
And love maintains it to the end.

Love cannot from its post withdraw;
Nor death, nor hell, nor sin, nor law,
Can turn the Surety's heart away;
He'll love His own to endless day.

Love has redeemed His sheep with blood;
And love will bring them safe to God;
Love calls them all from death to life;
And love will finish all their strife.

PILATE[21]

—

"What is truth?" John 18. 38

—

"What is truth?" It runs, you will observe, in the form of a personal question, that is, a question asked by one person of another. A question, therefore, of this kind implies two persons: the person who asks the question, and the person of whom the question is asked. Who, then, was the person who asked this important question: "What is truth?" Was he a good man? No. Was he a bad man? Why, if he was not a good man, he must have been a bad man; and yet, was he not the worst of men: at least, he was surrounded with, and hard pressed by worse men than he, for I think you will admit that to sin wilfully, is a greater sin than to sin ignorantly, and that the greater the privileges, the greater the crime of trampling them under foot. The man, then, who asked the question, if not the worst of men, was but a poor, weak, vacillating creature, ground down between fear of his master, Tiberius, a very monster of tyranny, cruelty, and cunning, and of the Jews, by whom he was surrounded, and that not merely the wayward, impetuous mob, but their leaders, the chief priests and elders, and all the council, who were thirsting after the blood of Jesus. Now, God was determined that His dear Son should be pronounced innocent of all charges by the very man in whose hands the administration of the law, at that time, lay. We read, therefore, that Pontius Pilate, the Roman governor, "took water, and washed his hands before the multitude, saying, I am innocent of the blood of this just Person: see ye to it." (See Matthew 27. 24). Thus, the very verdict of his own conscience was for saving Jesus, as an innocent Man, from a malefactor's death by crucifixion, if he could have done so without risking his own popularity and life. But, the purposes of God must stand, and the Scriptures be fulfilled. I need not tell you, then, that it was this very Pontius Pilate who asked the question: "What is truth?" And I need not tell you who it was of whom he asked it. Of no one less than the Son of God, who stood before His tribunal, that He might, according to the purposes of God, bear our sins in His own body on the tree. And yet, though he asked the question, he had no care or desire to hear the answer. It seems to have come out of his mouth in a sort of careless way, as if suggested to his mind by the Lord's words: "Every one that is of the truth heareth My voice." They fell upon his mind as something strange and new, and he therefore hastily asked, with a kind of careless infidelity: "What is truth?" Yet he seems to have been struck, either, with the majesty or the innocence of the Speaker, for we read: "And when he had said this, he went out again unto the Jews, and saith unto them, I find in Him no fault at all."

"I am," says Christ, "the Way";
Now, if we credit Him,
All other paths must lead astray,
How fair soe'er they seem.

"I am," says Christ, "the Truth";
Then all that lacks this test,
Proceed it from an angel's mouth,
Is but a lie at best.

"I am," says Christ, "the Life";
Let this be seen by faith,
It follows, without further strife,
That all besides is death.

If what those words aver,
The Holy Ghost apply,
The simplest Christian shall not err,
Nor be deceived, nor die.

THE DYING THIEF[22]

—

"Lord, remember me when Thou comest into Thy kingdom." Luke 23. 42.

—

God has given in His Word some astonishing instances of the freeness and sovereignty of His grace, but I do not know that we have a more striking instance than the one before us. It is true indeed that every called and saved vessel of mercy is an astonishing instance of the sovereignty of God's grace; and I believe every truly convinced sinner who is brought to the footstool of mercy, and made to receive salvation as a free gift, is convinced in his own experience that he himself is one of the most marvellous instances of sovereign grace. Yet there are several instances in the Scriptures that seem to shine forth with more distinguished lustre. For instance, look at the case of Paul, and compare it with that of the thief on the cross. I do think that all through the Scriptures we can scarcely find two more striking instances of the fulness and freeness of sovereign grace than these two. One a complete Pharisee, the other a thorough profligate. Which was farthest from heaven? We can scarcely say. Yet the same sovereign grace which could arrest the bloodthirsty Pharisee on his way to Damascus, was able also to snatch from death the expiring malefactor.

1. First, then, consider the *character of the man before grace called him. When* do you think grace called him? There are some people whose eyes, like owls and bats that cannot bear the full light of the sun, have been so dazzled by this glorious effulgence of sovereign grace that they have endeavoured to show that this man was not so bad as the other, and that there were some marks in his character which were not to be found in the other malefactor. In the saving of the one and in the leaving of the other there is such a display of God's electing decrees that these owls and bats could not bear its full lustre. But I think, if we compare the parallel places in the other Gospels, we shall find that the thief who was saved was not one whit better than he who perished. For we read, "The thieves also which were crucified with him cast the same in his teeth" (See Matthew 27. 44). So that it appears up to the moment when

sovereign grace touched this sinner's heart, he could unite with his brother thief in reviling, blaspheming, and casting reproaches on the Redeemer. "If thou be the Christ, save Thyself and us."

It would appear that this man who was being executed upon the cross for his crimes was not a common malefactor, but one of an extraordinary nature; for it seems that the Jews selected two of the vilest wretches they could pick out, in order to throw the greater disgrace on the Lord. So great was their enmity, so intense their hatred against the dear Son of God, that to cover Him with the lowest disgrace two malefactors were chosen, and He was put between them, as though they should thereby loudly declare, "Here are three criminals, and the One in the middle the worst of the three." But there is another reason why we may suppose both were hardened characters. In those days, history tells us that Judaea was much infested with highwaymen. and these two men seem to have been companions of Barabbas, of whom we read, "And there was one named Barabbas, which lay bound with them that had made insurrection with him, who had committed murder in the insurrection" (see Mark 15. 7). Then here we have a hardened malefactor, a wretch who was justly dying upon the cross.

2. Observe *the sovereignty of God's grace calling him.* Try to represent to your mind these two malefactors, each on the side of the Lord Jesus Christ, reviling and blaspheming with their tongues, and thus hoping to find some little relief in railing upon the Lord of life and glory. Well, can you see any difference here? These two men are writhing on the cross, a few hours will close the scene, here is a hell opening her jaws to receive them, here is the wrath of God ready to burst forth. What should there be in one man more than in the other? Nothing, absolutely nothing. Why, then, did one pray, and the other not pray? How is it one was called, and the other left? Why, wholly and solely—let men cavil and blaspheme as they may —because sovereign grace interposed, and God's electing decrees were carried out in the salvation of one and the ruin of the other. But then someone might say, "Was not God unjust?" How can that be? Would not God's justice have left them *both to* perish? But His mercy interfered in the behalf of His child, whom He had decreed

57

eternally thus to call and save.

3. Look a little at *his character after he was called by grace.* This is a very important point. The man was not saved and taken to heaven without a change. The words of the Lord must ever stand: "Except a man be born again, he cannot see the kingdom of God" (see John 3. 3). Thus this dying thief must have had a new birth, that mighty revolution wrought in his soul, or else he never could have been with Jesus in Paradise. Regenerating grace touched his heart, the scales dropped from his eyes, the veil of unbelief was taken from his heart, faith was given him, and repentance unto life.

> Ah! but for free and sovereign grace,
> I still had lived estranged from God,
> Till hell had proved the destined place
> Of my deserved but dread abode.
>
> But O, amazed, I see the hand
> That stopped me in my wild career;
> A miracle of grace I stand;
> The Lord has taught my heart to fear.
>
> To fear His name, to trust His grace,
> To learn His will be my employ;
> Till I shall see Him face to face,
> Himself my heaven, Himself my joy.

THE NEW TESTAMENT CHURCHES[23]

—

"Ye received the Word of God, ...not as the word of men, but as it is in truth, the Word of God." 1 Thessalonians 2. 13.

—

If we examine the features of the New Testament Churches as reflected in the Inspired Page, and seek to gather from that mode of internal evidence, the spiritual condition of each, we shall find that, though in Christ Jesus all were one, yet in grace and gift, in state and standing, in knowledge and experience, in walk and conduct they widely differed from one another. Thus, the Church at Rome seems to have been distinguished above her sister Churches for the strength of her faith. "I thank my God," says the apostle, "through Jesus Christ for you all, that your faith is spoken of throughout the whole world." (See Romans 1. 8). So conspicuous and eminent was the faith of the Roman believers, that they had become an object of universal mention and thankfulness among the churches. And this seems to be one reason why the apostle, in his epistle to the Romans, dwells so fully and largely upon justification, they being able, above other Churches, to enter experimentally into the glorious doctrine of justification by faith in the righteousness of the Son of God. Thus the whole Church, to the end of time, profits by the strength of their faith; for, had they been weak in faith, they could not have received an epistle so fully declaring the way whereby a sinner stands justified before God, by the imputation of the obedience of Christ, without the works of the law. The Corinthian Church was particularly favoured with the gifts of utterance and knowledge, as the apostle declares: "I thank my God always on your behalf, for the grace of God which is given you by Jesus Christ; that in everything ye are enriched by Him in all utterance, and in all knowledge; Even as the testimony of Christ was confirmed in you: So that ye come behind in no gift; waiting for the coming of the Lord Jesus Christ:" (See 1 Corinthians 1. 4-7). These gifts indeed had their attendant perils, for we find the apostle warning them against being puffed up thereby, and assuring them that they might speak with the tongues of men and of angels, have the gift of prophecy, and understand all mysteries and all knowledge, and yet be nothing. (See 1 Corinthians 8. 1; 13. 2). The Galatian Churches

59

had, unhappily, become "removed from Him that called" them "into the grace of Christ unto another gospel:" which the apostle declares was really "not another," as not being worthy of the name of gospel, but was a perversion of the gospel of Christ. (See Galatians 1. 6, 7). They had thus strayed from the green pastures and still waters of gospel grace, and got upon the barren heath of legal service; had left the warm sunshine of Mount Zion, and become entangled in the smoke of Mount Sinai. The Church at Philippi was suffering under persecution, for to it we read, was, "given in the behalf of Christ, not only to believe on Him but, also to suffer for His sake;" (see Philippians 1. 29); and yet it continued firm in "the fellowship" of "the gospel from the first day until now." (See Philippians 1. 5). There was also, in it, a great spirit of love and liberality; for no Church communicated with Paul, as concerning giving and receiving, but it only. (See Philippians 4. 15). The wealthy Corinthians allowed him to preach to them the gospel of God, freely, suffering the poorer Church at Philippi to supply that which was lacking to him (see 2 Corinthians 11. 7-9); proving, as is often the case, the greater willingness of the poor, than of the rich, to give to the cause and servants of God. The Churches of Ephesus and of Colosse seem to have been further advanced in knowledge, and more fully and firmly established in the truth, than most of the other New Testament Churches, the former especially having had the benefit of Paul's personal ministry for three years. They were, therefore, better qualified to receive those deep epistles which were severally addressed to them, in which the grandest and most glorious mysteries of our most holy faith are unfolded with a wisdom and a power which seem to leave us ever learners, and never able to grasp them fully, to our satisfaction. The Church at Thessalonica, was inferior to that at Rome, in faith, to that of Corinth, in gifts, to that at Ephesus, in knowledge, and yet was one of the most favoured in the New Testament. The two epistles which Paul sent them were the first which ever issued from his pen, and were written to them in the early days of their profession, about a year after the gospel had come to them not "in word only, but also in power, and in the Holy Ghost, and in much assurance." They had been much persecuted for righteousness' sake, and had "received the word in much affliction, with joy of the Holy Ghost." (See I Thessalonians 1. 5, 6). There was, also, one feature in their Christian character which shone forth with distinguished lustre—*brotherly love*—according to the apostle's own testimony: "But as touching brotherly love ye need not that I write unto you: for ye yourselves are taught of God to love one another." (See 1 Thessalonians 4. 9). Blessed mark of heavenly grace! The apostle also seems to have been peculiarly attached to them, for he says: "So being affectionately desirous of you, we were willing to have imparted unto you, not the gospel of God only, but also our own souls, because ye were dear unto us." (See 1 Thessalonians 2. 8). The reason of his great love to them appears to have been, first, the power which he felt in his own soul in preaching to them the word of life, for he calls to their mind, "ye know what manner of men we were among you for your sake;" and, secondly, the way in which they received the Word from his lips, which made him say: "For what is our hope, or joy, or crown of rejoicing? Are not even ye in the presence of our Lord Jesus Christ at His coming? For ye are our glory and joy." (See 1 Thessalonians 2. 19, 20). When we look at the character of this eminent apostle of the Gentiles, as drawn, as if unconsciously, by his own pen, what a pattern, what an example he sets for Christian ministers! How his whole soul was in the work! What ardent love to the souls of men! What singleness of eye to the glory of God! How delighted he was to find power attending the gospel he preached, and a harvest of living souls falling beneath the sickle of the Word, as he thrust it into the crop! We may, perhaps, say that four things gladdened Paul's heart in finding the power of God resting so abundantly upon His Word: 1, the glory of God, which was, above all things, dear to his soul; 2, the exaltation of the Lord Jesus Christ in His Person and work; 3, the rich harvest of souls gathered by his instrumentality; and, 4, the seals and evidences afforded thereby of his being a servant of God, an apostle of Jesus Christ. O! that the Lord would raise up men after His own heart, upon whom some measure of the spirit, that we see in Paul, might rest; men blessed with his simplicity and godly sincerity, favoured with his singleness of eye to the glory of God and the exaltation of the Lord Jesus, and whose speech and preaching, like his, might be "not with enticing words of man's wisdom, but in demonstration of the Spirit and of power." Then, indeed, we should see that the faith of those who received their testimony would stand, not in the wisdom of men, but in the power of God. (See 1 Corinthians 2. 4, 5).

Ye souls, redeemed with blood,
And called by grace divine,
Walk worthy of your God,
And let your conduct shine;
Keep Christ, your living Head, in view,
In all you say, in all you do.

Has Jesus made you free?
Then you are free indeed;
Ye sons of liberty,
Ye chosen royal seed,
Walk worthy of your Lord, and view
Your glorious Head, in all you do.

Shall sons of heavenly birth
Their dignity debase?
Unite with sons of earth,
And take a servant's place?
The slaves to sin and Satan too?
Forget to keep their Lord in view?

Forbid it, mighty God!
Preserve us in Thy fear;
Uphold with staff and rod,
And guard from every snare;
Teach us to walk with Christ in view,
And honour Him in all we do.

Increase our faith and love,
And make us watch and pray;
O fix our souls above,
Nor let us ever stray;
Dear Lord, do Thou our strength renew,
And lead us on with Christ in view.

THE WRITERS OF THE EPISTLES[24]

—

"All Scripture is given by inspiration of God, …" 2 Timothy 3. 16.

—

The various writers of the Epistles of the New Testament, though all equally inspired of God, though they all preach the same doctrine, unfold the same experience, and enforce the same practice, yet differ widely in their mode of setting forth divine truths. Thus Paul shines conspicuously in setting forth the grand doctrines of the gospel, such as the union of the Church, as chosen in Christ, with her great covenant Head, salvation by free, sovereign, distinguishing, and superabounding grace, justification by faith in the Son of God, and the blessed and abundant fruits and privileges which spring out of the relationship of the Church to God from her union with the Son of His love. It was necessary for the instruction. edification, and cons-olation of the Church of God that these grand and glorious truths should be not only revealed in the gospel, and preached by the Apostles, but be put upon permanent record for all ages as a part of the inspired Scriptures. God, therefore chose Paul and endowed him with the largest of intellects, the greatest amount of grace, and the fullest possession of the gifts of the Holy Ghost which perhaps ever met in any one man. Thus to him was given to write the greater part of the inspired Epistles of the New Testament.

James keeps on lower ground. He does not soar into those sublime heights in which his brother Paul found himself borne up and sustained with his strong pinion; but directing his pen against the perversions of Paul's gospel, which had crept into the Churches, and aiming his keen arrows against the Antinomians of his day, shows that there was no use talking about being justified by faith without works, if they meant thereby to exclude works altogether from having part or lot in the ministry of the gospel or the walk of a believer; and that it would not do to say if men only believed in Christ they might live as they listed, without paying the least regard to doing the will of God, or bringing forth the fruits of righteousness. All this loose, licentious, Antinomian doctrine, James cuts up root and branch.

Peter, melted and mellowed in the furnace of affliction, writes as one who had experienced much inward conflict, and therefore deals much with the trials, temptations, and sufferings of the Church of God; yet looks with steady eye, and points with clear pen, to the glory which is to be revealed, that shall make amends for all.

Jude bursts forth into a stern and severe denunciation against the ungodly men, who, in his day, had abused the grand truths of gospel grace to walk after their own lusts. He points his keen pen against "the spots in their feasts of charity," that would seem in those days to have sprung up to defile the clean garments which should have been worn at such holy celebrations of the love and blood of the Lamb. He denounces the judgment of God against the "trees twice dead, plucked up by the roots;" "the clouds without water, and the wandering stars, to whom was reserved the blackness of darkness for ever."

When we come to John, we seem to come into a different atmosphere–an atmosphere of love and holiness. He in his youth had laid his head upon the Redeemer's bosom, and there had drunk in large and deep draughts of love. He had stood by Him when upon the cross, had witnessed His agonies, heard His dying words, and seen the spear of the Roman soldier pierce His heart, so that out of it came blood and water. It seems, therefore, as if the reflection of what he had thus tasted, felt, and handled, tinged as it were his Epistle with golden light. If I may use a figure, it seems almost to resemble what we see on a summer eve, when the setting sun sheds a bright glow of golden light upon every object; or if I may borrow an illustration from art as well as nature, as we see it transferred to the canvas of great painters, such as Claude or Turner, where every object seems lit up with this golden beam. Thus when we come to this Epistle, it seems as if a ray of golden light, the light of holiness and love, spread itself over every word and bathed it with the hues of heaven. It is this peculiar atmosphere of love and holiness which makes every word of this Epistle so full of light, life, and power.

Standing then as if upon this high and holy ground, and breathing this heavenly air, this atmosphere of purity and love, the disciple whom Jesus loved sends a warning voice to the children of God in the words of our text, and solemnly cautions them against the love of the world. He knew their propensity, what was in the heart of man, and that though the saints of God were redeemed by the blood of Christ, taught by His Spirit, and wrought upon by His grace, yet still there was in them a carnal, earthly principle, which cleaved to, and loved the world. He therefore lifts up a warning voice: "Love not the world, neither the things that are in the world." And to shew that this was not a matter of small importance, but involved in it life or death, he goes on to testify that whatever profession a man might make, if he really loved the world, the love of the Father was not in his heart. He then takes a rapid view of all that was in the world, and summing it up under three heads, as the lust of the flesh, the lust of the eyes, and the pride of life, passes upon it this condemning sentence, that it is not of the Father, but of the world. He then lifts up in still stronger strain his warning voice, that the world is passing away and the lust thereof, and that there will be a speedy end to all this show and glitter. But he adds, to encourage those who, in spite of all opposition, are doing the will of God, that when all things here below shall pass away and perish, they shall abide for ever.

Father of mercies, in Thy Word
What endless glory shines!
For ever be Thy Name adored
For these celestial lines.

Here may the wretched sons of want,
Exhaustless riches find;
Riches above what earth can grant,
And lasting as the mind.

Here the fair tree of knowledge grows
And yields a free repast;
Sublimer sweets than nature knows
Invite the longing taste.

Here the Redeemer's welcome voice
Spreads heavenly peace around;
And life, and everlasting joys,
Attend the blissful sound.

O may these heavenly pages be
My ever dear delight;
And still new beauties may I see,
And still increasing light.

Divine Instructor, gracious Lord,
Be Thou for ever near;
Teach me to love Thy sacred Word,
And view my Saviour there.

JOHN, THE APOSTLE (1)[25]

—

"… the disciple whom Jesus loved." John 21. 20.

—

The life of John, the beloved disciple, was, by the express wisdom and goodness of God, prolonged beyond the space allotted to his fellow apostles. Church history informs us that he lived to be nearly one hundred years old; and Jerome, one of the ancient Church Fathers, as quoted by Milner, records a pleasing incident of him at that advanced period of life, which is so much in harmony with his general character, that it seems to deserve our credence better than most of the current traditions concerning him. It is this. When he was too old and infirm to walk, he was carried into the assemblies of the Christians at Ephesus, and there he confined himself to these few simple words of exhortation: "Beloved, let us love one another:". But I intimated that it was by the express wisdom and goodness of God that his life was so long spared; and now I will tell you my reason for drawing this conclusion. Satan, when he found he could not overthrow the Church of Christ by violence, changed his plan, and sought to subvert it by treachery. He therefore raised up in almost all directions, where there were Churches of Christ, a set of vile characters, men erroneous in doctrine and ungodly in life, who sprang up as tares in the fields of wheat. To us it seems scarcely credible that, within thirty or forty years after our Lord's death and resurrection, there should start up in the Churches such characters as Jude and Peter describe with their graphic pens. Hear Jude's description of many members of Christian Churches in his day, which, taking the Bible date of the epistle, A.D. 66, was but 33 years after the ascension of Jesus—a shorter space of time than I have professed to be a servant of Christ. "For there are certain men crept in unawares, who were before of old ordained to this condemnation, ungodly men, turning the grace of our God into lasciviousness, and denying the only Lord God, and our Lord Jesus Christ." "These," he adds, "are spots in your feasts of charity, when they feast with you, feeding themselves without fear: clouds they are without water, carried about of winds; trees whose fruit withereth, without fruit, twice dead, plucked up by the roots; Raging waves of the sea,

66

foaming out their own shame; wandering stars, to whom is reserved the blackness of darkness for ever." (See Jude 4, 12, 13). What strong, what emphatic language! And yet the Church of Christ, at that early period, was pestered with these infamous characters. You will find equally strong language concerning them in the Second Epistle of Peter, written about the same time. And even Paul, a year or two before the same period, denounces similar characters in terms not much less severe: "For many walk, of whom I have told you often, and now tell you even weeping, that they are the enemies of the cross of Christ: Whose end is destruction, whose God is their belly, and whose glory is in their shame, who mind earthly things." (See Philippians 3. 18, 19). And again: "For there are many unruly and vain talkers and deceivers, specially they of the circumcision: Whose mouths must be stopped, who subvert whole houses, teaching things which they ought not, for filthy lucre's sake. They profess that they know God; but in works they deny Him, being abominable, and disobedient, and unto every good work reprobate." (See Titus 1. 10, 11, 16).

Now, what a mercy it was that John should have been spared to witness, not only the introduction of these ungodly characters into the professing Church, but their full development; that he, who had been an eye-witness of the Lord's glory on the mount of transfiguration; who had viewed His agony in the garden; who had stood by Him when expiring on the cross, and marked the blood and water gush from His pierced side; who had seen and handled Him after the resurrection, and had beheld His ascension from Bethany, should have been spared to witness all these evils introduced into the primitive Churches; for he was thus enabled, towards the close of his life, by the grace of God and the inspiration of the Holy Ghost, to testify, with all the greater power and authority as an eye-witness, against these evils and these errors. The "grievous wolves," for instance, that Paul prophesied should enter in among them at Ephesus (see Acts 20. 29) were there before his eyes, "not sparing the flock." And so with other Churches, such as Pergamos and Thyatira. The men and their evil ways and works were not shadows in the future, like the beast with seven heads and ten horns, but were then living, moving, and working in the Churches with all their craft and hypocrisy, all their errors and heresies, all their wantonness and wickedness. God, therefore, preserved him so long in life that, as his last New Testament witness, he might deliver a standing testimony against those errors and evils which afflicted the early Churches. If we had a fuller knowledge of these errors and evils, we should see that John's testimony was particularly directed against them. We should see why he was specially led in his gospel to testify so plainly to the Deity and eternal Sonship of Jesus, truths which these heretics denied; and to preserve, so carefully, the exact discourses of the blessed Lord, in which He asserted His essential oneness with the Father as the Son of God, and yet the reality of His flesh and blood as the Son of man. So, in his epistles, and especially in the first and longest of them, we should see how, in every verse, he denounces some vile error, or declares some important truth. Well may we say that upon it are inscribed, as with a ray of light, these three conspicuous features: Truth, holiness, and love. How, for instance, he testifies for the *Truth,* by setting before us the essential Deity, the eternal Sonship, and the propitiation made for sin by our blessed Lord! How he treats of His advocacy with the Father, as Jesus Christ the righteous, and assures us that His blood cleanseth from all sin! How he denounces error with most trenchant pen, cutting off those who hold it, as men devoid of the grace of God, and bidding us take heed of them, and not even receive them into our houses, or bid them God speed! And is not *holiness* the very breath of the epistle? How he tells us that he who is blessed with a good hope through grace of seeing Jesus as He is, purifies himself, even as He is pure! (See 1 John 3. 3). How he warns us against loving the world, or the things that are in the world! (See 1 John 2. 15). How he seeks to lead us up to have "fellowship … with the Father and … his Son Jesus Christ" (see 1 John 1. 3); declares that, "He that saith he abideth in Him ought himself also so to walk, even as He walked;"! and lays it down as a practical test of the new birth: "If ye know that He is righteous, ye know that every one that doeth righteousness is born of Him." (See 1 John 2. 29). Nor need I say with what a glorious flood of heavenly *love* this epistle is bathed. The love of God, in Christ, to us, in sending His Son to be the propitiation for our sins; the love of Christ in laying down His life for us; the love which we should have to Him and to each other—is not this divine and heavenly love in its fountain and its streams, in its communication and in its claims, in its living fruits and practical effects, the very animating breath of the whole epistle? The love of God, softening and melting his heart, seems to have touched his pen as with a double measure of holy force and fire, so that we may almost say, if Truth be the body, and holiness the soul, love is the spirit of this blessed epistle.

JOHN, THE APOSTLE (2)[26]

—

"But ye have an unction from the Holy One, …" 1 John 2. 20.

—

The life of John, the beloved disciple, was prolonged to a very late period; and we see the wisdom and goodness of God in thus prolonging his life, that he might be a standing bulwark against the errors and heresies which overflowed the primitive Church. When the Lord of life and glory was upon earth, all the bent of Satan's malice was against him; but when, according to God's elect purpose and counsel, Satan had put it into the heart of Judas to betray Christ into the hands of the Jews, and the Son of God was nailed to the accursed tree (for Satan was outwitted by his own invention, and outshot by his own bow); then, when Jesus had ascended into heaven, all the power of Satan was turned against His disciples. When he could not touch the Head, he aimed his arrows at the members; and no sooner did the Lord pour out upon the Church the gift of the Holy Ghost in great measure on the day of Pentecost, than Satan immediately introduced all manner of error and heresy to harass the Church. Now, through the kind providence of God, the life of John was prolonged to bear testimony against these errors and heresies; and thus this blessed apostle was a standing testimony against the errors that came in like a flood.

In the chapter from which the text is taken, John addresses himself to the Church of God as divided into three distinct classes. There are the weak and young, whom he calls "little children." There are those who are established in the divine life through exercises, trials, temptations, and through corresponding blessings; these he calls "young men." And there are those whose lives are verging upon eternity, who have received many testimonies of God's goodness and lovingkindness, and have thus become "fathers."

Speaking, then, to the Church of God as thus composed, he puts them in mind of those seducers and heretics who had crept into the Church. He says: "Little children, it is the last time:" (that is the last dispensation); "and as ye have heard that antichrist shall come, even now are there many antichrists." They had heard of antichrist, and they supposed that antichrist was some single person; the man of sin that was to rise. "No," says the apostle: "there are many antichrists." All that are opposed to Christ, all that deny the story of His Person, the efficacy of His work, and the power of His blood, these are antichrists, because they are all against Christ. Now these antichrists were formerly among them, members of their Churches, walking, apparently, in Christian fellowship. The apostle therefore says: "They went out from us, but they were not of us." They could not receive the love of the Truth, because their hearts secretly loathed it. They could not endure Christian experience, because they possessed it not, nor could they submit to gospel precepts and Christian discipline, because their affections went out after the world. The Truth of God, the pure Truth, did not suit their impure, corrupt minds, so they went out from the Church, they separated themselves, and thus abandoned the communion and community of the faithful, for, "if they had been of us," in heart and soul, knit together in the bonds of the Spirit, in real spiritual union and communion, if they had thus "been of us, they would no doubt have continued with us: but they went out, that they might be made manifest that they were not all of us." Separating from the company of God's people is a testimony that such are not of God's people, and they make it manifest that they never were, in heart and soul, united with the family of God when they withdraw themselves from them. But the apostle would here rather infer: "How came it to be otherwise with you?" What has preserved you faithful, when others have proved unfaithful? What has kept you still leaning on and looking unto a crucified Immanuel, when others have trampled on His blood, and turned after idols? Was it your own wisdom, your own ability, your own righteousness, your own strength? No; not so: "But ye have an unction from the Holy One; and ye know all things." This is what he implies: "Ye have an unction from the Holy One." It is that which has kept you, it is that which has taught you. "Ye little children," "young men," and "fathers," "ye have an unction from the Holy One," and, by that unction, "ye know all things."

Blest Spirit of truth, eternal God,
Thou meek and lowly Dove,
Who fill'st the soul through Jesus' blood,
With faith, and hope, and love;

Who comfortest the heavy heart,
By sin and sorrow pressed;
Who to the dead canst life impart,
And to the weary rest;

Thy sweet communion charms the soul,
And gives true peace and joy,
Which Satan's power cannot control,
Nor all his wiles destroy;

Come from the blissful realms above;
Our longing breasts inspire
With Thy soft flames of heavenly love,
And fan the sacred fire.

Let no false comfort lift us up
To confidence that's vain;
Nor let their faith and courage droop,
For whom the Lamb was slain.

Breathe comfort where distress abounds,
Make the whole conscience clean,
And heal, with balm from Jesus' wounds,
The festering sores of sin.

Vanquish our lust, our pride remove,
Take out the heart of stone;
Show us the Father's boundless love,
And merits of the Son.

The Father sent the Son to die;
The willing Son obeyed;
The witness Thou, to ratify
The purchase Christ has made.

SAUL OF TARSUS[27]

—

"And such were some of you." 1 Corinthians 6. 11

—

What reason the Church of Christ has to bless God for the epistles that issued from Paul's inspired pen! And though it may seem scarcely right to select one epistle more than another as pregnant with heavenly instruction, yet, I think, we may safely say, that the epistles to the Romans, to the Galatians, and to the Hebrews, have, of all the epistles, been most signally blessed to the Church of the living God. And when, for a moment, we contrast their author, Paul the apostle, with Saul of Tarsus, O how striking, how miraculous was the change that grace made in him!

Let us take our thoughts backward to three particular seasons in the life of Saul of Tarsus. View him, first, at the feet of Gamaliel, imbibing from his lips that traditionary law, that code of rites and ceremonies, which forms, at the present day, the religion of Israel. Had it then been whispered in his ear: The time will come when you will declare these things to be "weak and beggarly elements," trample them under your feet, and scatter them to the four winds of heaven, would not that youth have said: Perish the thought!

Move a step further in the life of Saul of Tarsus. View him working out his own righteousness, striving to set up a religion whereby he could please God, and force his way to heaven. Had one then whispered in his ear: The time will come when all your hope will rest upon justification by the obedience of another, he would have said: That time never will come; the sun may as well cease to rise as for me to look to another's righteousness whereby to be justified.

Take one step further, and view him keeping the clothes of the witnesses, who had stripped themselves, lest their loose garments might encumber them, while they were, according to the Mosaic law, to throw the first stone at Stephen. Had one then whispered in his ear: The time will come when you will believe in Jesus of Nazareth, and die for His Name, would not the thought of his heart have been: Let me rather die first, than that such an event should ever come to pass? But, doubtless, these very circumstances in Paul's life were

72

mysteriously overruled for the profit of the Church of God. For he, having been in these states, has been able to trace out with clearer evidence, and more powerful argument, the truth as it is in Jesus, from having experimentally known both sides of the question.

Ye souls redeemed by Jesus' blood,
Salvation's theme pursue;
Exalt the sovereign grace of God,
For "such were some of you!"

From head to foot defiled by sin,
Deep in rebellion too;
This awful state mankind are in,
"And such were some of you!"

Whilst they are sinners dead to God,
Ye highly favoured few
Are washed from sin by Jesus' blood;
For "such were some of you!"

As ye are chosen from the rest,
To grace the praise is due;
Be sovereign love for ever blest,
For "such were some of you!"

PAUL (1)[28]

—

"For by grace are ye saved …" Ephesians 2. 8.

—

Look at Paul. Where can we find, among the sons of men, a parallel to the great apostle of the Gentiles? What a large capacity! What a powerful intellect he naturally possessed, but how subdued and subjugated it became by grace, and how devoted to the glory of God and the advancement of the kingdom of His dear Son! How grace arrested him at Damascus gate, cast him down, body and soul, at the Redeemer's feet, translated him from the power of darkness into the kingdom of God's dear Son, and changed a bloodthirsty persecutor of the Church of Christ into a minister and an apostle, the greatest ever seen! As such, what deep humility, thorough disinterestedness, noble simplicity, godly zeal, unwearied labours, distinguished him from first to last—a course of more than thirty years! How, in his inspired writings, he pours, as it were, from his pen the richest streams of heavenly truth! With what clearness, power, and savour he describes and enforces the way of salvation through the bloodshedding and obedience of the Son of God, the blessings of free grace, the glorious privileges of the saints, and the things that make for their happiness and holiness! How, in every epistle, it seems as if his pen could hardly drop a line without, in some way, setting forth the infinite grace, the boundless mercy, and unfathomable love of God, as displayed in the gift of His dear Son, and the blessings that flow to the Church through His blood and love.

But look not at Paul only. View the jewels, on every side, that grace has set in the Redeemer's crown, out of the most depraved and abject materials! Who, for instance, were these Ephesians to whom Paul wrote this wonderful epistle? The most foolish and besotted of idolators, so infatuated with their image which fell down from Jupiter—most probably some huge meteoric stone, that had fallen from the sky—that they spent two hours, until they wearied out their throats, with crying: "Great is Diana of the Ephesians!"—men debased with every lust, ripe and ready for every crime. How rich, how marvellous the grace that changed worshippers of Diana into worshippers of Jehovah, brutal howlers into singers who made melody in their heart to the Lord (see Ephesians 5. 19), and magicians, full of "curious arts" and Satanic witchcraft, into saints built upon the foundation of the apostles and prophets!

Now, cannot the same grace, that did so much for them, do the same or similar things for us? Is the nature of man now, less vile, or is the grace of Christ now, less full and free? Has the lapse of 1800 years raised man out of the depths of the fall, eradicated sin from his constitution, cleansed the foul leprosy of his nature, and purified it into holiness? Let the thin sheet of decent morality and civilisation be taken off the corpse, and there it lies in all its hideous ghastliness. Human nature is still what it ever was—dead in trespasses and sins. Or, has time, which changes so many things on earth, changed things in heaven? Is not God the same gracious Father, Jesus the same compassionate Saviour, the Holy Spirit the same heavenly Teacher? Is not the gospel the same glad tidings of salvation, and the power of the gospel the same to every one that believeth? Then why should not we be blessed with the same spiritual blessings as the saints at Ephesus? Why may not the same Jesus be to us what He was to them—the same Spirit to do for us and in us, what He did for and in them—and the same grace save and sanctify us, which saved and sanctified them? Here, and here alone, is our strength, our help, our hope, our all.

PAUL (2)[29]

Every saved sinner is a miracle of grace; and I believe, in my very heart and conscience, that the Lord will make every saved sinner know, feel, and acknowledge it; for He will give him, from time to time, such deep discoveries of what he is in the Adam fall, as will convince him, beyond all question, and all controversy, that nothing but the rich, sovereign, distinguishing, and superabounding grace of God can save his soul from the bottomless pit. But, though this is true in the case of every vessel of mercy, yet, as if to establish our faith more clearly and fully in the sovereignty of grace, the Lord has given us two special instances in the Scriptures wherein the miracles of His grace seem to shine forth in the most distinguished lustre and glory; and, as if to make the contrast greater, they are of two characters exactly opposite. Yet the grace of God shines so conspicuously in both, that I hardly know to which I can assign the preference. These two characters are—one, the thief upon the cross; the other, Saul of Tarsus. Let us view them separately.

First, I look at the thief upon the cross. I see there a hardened malefactor, the associate of ruffians, the accomplice of murderers, for he was, no doubt, one of the gang of Barabbas, and selected, when he was spared, as one of the worst, to stamp the Redeemer's crucifixion by his side with the deeper ignominy. I trace him, then, through his life of violence and crime, and see him imbruing his hands in the blood of the innocent. I see him, year after year, sinning to the utmost stretch of all his faculties, until at last brought to suffer condign punishment for his crimes against the laws of his fellow man. I see him amidst all his sufferings, at first joining his brother thief in blaspheming the Lamb of God, who was hanging between them upon the cross; for I read that: "the *thieves* also that were crucified with Him cast the same in His teeth." (See Matthew 27. 44). But the appointed time arrives, the predestinated moment strikes, and I see the grace of God, as a lightning flash, not to destroy, but to save, enter into his heart, as if just at the last gasp, to snatch him from the gates of death and the very jaws of hell. I see it communicate to his soul, conviction of sin and repentance of his crimes, for he acknowledged them to God and man. I see how the Holy Ghost raised up, in that dying malefactor's soul, a faith in the Person, work, kingdom, grace, and power of the Son of God—a faith so strong, that I can hardly find a parallel to it, unless in that of Abraham offering up his son Isaac as a burnt offering. When the very disciples forsook Him and fled; when His cruel enemies were celebrating their highest triumph; when earth shook to its centre, and the sun withdrew its light; at the lowest depths of the Redeemers shame and sorrow—O, miracle of grace!—here was a poor, dying thief acknowledging Jesus as King in Zion, and praying: "Lord, remember me when Thou comest into Thy kingdom." O, my soul, hast thou not prayed the same prayer to the same King of kings and Lord of lords?

But now I turn and see another character. I view a man trained up in the strictest form of religion then known, living the most austere, upright, unblemished life. I see him repeating prayer after prayer, and making vow after vow, ever setting before his eyes, day after day, the law of Moses, and directing by that, his life and conduct. I next see him, in the height of zeal, ravaging the Church of God as a wolf devastates a fold, till satiated with blood. I see him holding the garments of the witnesses against the martyred Stephen. I view him rejoicing, as with fiendish joy, as stone after stone was fiercely hurled, and fell with crushing violence upon the martyr's head. But O, what a change! I see him now fallen to the earth at Damascus gate, under the power of that light from heaven, above the brightness of the sun, which shone round about him; and I hear him saying, all trembling and astonished: "Lord, what wilt Thou have me to do?" (See Acts 9. 6). Freewill, wert thou at Damascus gate? Wert thou not hurrying him on to deeds of blood? Was he not doing thy bidding when he was breathing out threatenings and slaughter against the disciples of the Lord? Did thy voice arrest his hand? Free grace, was not the conquest wholly, solely thine? Now, can you tell me which of these two saved sinners shall carry the palm the highest, or sing the song the loudest? Can you, ye saints of God, decide in which of these two men the grace of God shines forth the more conspicuously? Was it in touching the heart of the malefactor on the cross, or that of the hardened pharisee? I freely confess I can hardly pronounce an opinion, for my mind hovers between the two; but, of the two, I should give Paul the preference, for, to bring down the proud, self-satisfied, self-righteous pharisee, seems almost a greater miracle of grace than to convert a dying malefactor, especially when we take into account what the grace of God afterwards made him, and how it wrought in him to be such a saint and such an apostle. To show what grace taught and made him, we need go no farther than this very chapter. I see here what the grace of God did in this man's heart, and, as I read the blessed record of his experience, as here it poured itself forth in a stream of life and feeling from his very soul, I read in every line—I might say in every word—what a mighty revolution must have been wrought in him, to make him now so dearly love that Jesus whom he had once abhorred, that, for His sake he counted all things but dung that he might know, win, and be found in Him, and that the righteousness he had once despised, he now felt was his only justification before, and his only acceptance with, God.

"Gaius whom I love in the Truth." 3 John 2. 20.

—

The third epistle of John differs from most of the other epistles of the New Testament, in being written to an individual—to "the well-beloved Gaius," of whom we read elsewhere: "Gaius mine host, and of the whole church, saluteth you." This Gaius appears to have been a man of a very enlarged heart towards the children of God; for he was not satisfied with being the host of Paul, and entertaining him kindly, but his house and heart were both large enough to entertain the whole Church of God at Corinth.

To this open-hearted and affectionate Gaius, John, the apostle, addresses his third epistle: "The elder unto the well-beloved Gaius, whom I love in the truth." There was a difference in the form of the letters among the ancients, compared with that observed by ourselves. Their custom was, not as ours, to put the name of the writer at the *end* of the epistle, but they placed his name at the *beginning;* and, next in order, the name of the person to whom it was addressed. We have an instance of this in the Acts of the Apostles, where we have an original letter preserved, which Claudius Lysias sent to Felix. He commences thus: "Claudius Lysias, unto the most excellent governor Felix, sendeth greeting." This was the form of letter customary among the ancients. Claudius Lysias was the writer; he therefore puts his own name first. The most excellent governor, Felix, was the person to whom the letter was sent; his name comes next. But, besides this, it was the usual custom to add at the beginning, a friendly greeting, the writer wishing his correspondent "health,"—what we should call something complimentary. We find the Apostle Paul following this prevailing custom in all his epistles. He first puts his own name, and next, that of the Church or persons to whom he wrote; and then offers prayers to God that He would bless them with mercy, grace, and truth. It was the custom then, at the beginning of the letter, to offer some short desire for the health of the correspondent, that being the greatest temporal blessing the writer could wish for his friend. We find the apostle, John, following this custom; and, being a spiritual man, and writing a spiritual letter to a spiritual friend, he gives the usual salutation a spiritual turn. He does not write as a carnal writer would do: The elder unto the well-beloved Gaius, health—which was the usual form; but he gives this desire for his health a spiritual turn: "Beloved, I wish above all things that thou mayest prosper and be in health, even as thy soul prospereth." It is as though he should say: I wish thee temporal health, if it be the Lord's will; but, far more, I wish thee spiritual health. I wish thy circumstances to prosper, and thy body to be in health, as far as God sees fit to bestow; but only so far as is consistent with the health of thy soul. I wish it even as thy soul prospereth. As though again he should say: I cannot wish thee temporal prosperity, if it be not good for thy spiritual welfare. But, if thy soul prospers and be in health, with this, then, I can wish thee temporal prosperity and bodily health.

How sweet, how heavenly is the sight,
When those that love the Lord,
In one another's peace delight,
And so fulfil his word!

When each can feel his brother's sigh,
And with him bear a part;
When sorrow flows from eye to eye,
And joy from heart to heart.

When free from envy, scorn, and pride,
Our wishes all above,
Each can his brother's failings hide,
And show a brother's love.

When love in one delightful stream
Through every bosom flows;
When union sweet and dear esteem,
In every action glows!

Love is the golden chain that binds
The happy souls above;
And he's an heir of heaven that finds
His bosom glow with love.

THE LAMB'S WIFE

—

"Let us be glad and rejoice, and give honour to him: for the marriage of the Lamb is come, and his wife hath made herself ready." Revelation 19. 7

—

What a mercy—a mercy beyond all expression, and indeed all conception, it is to have a religion which will take us to heaven; which will not leave us in the agony of death, but will be with us in that solemn hour, carry us in peace through the dark and gloomy valley—dark and gloomy to the flesh, and land us safe in the glorious presence of God. Now no religion either can or will do this but that which is wrought in the soul by the power of God Himself. We want two things to take us to heaven: a title to it, and a meetness for it. Our only title to heaven is the blood and righteousness of the Son of God—that blood which "cleanseth from all sin," and that right-eousness which "justifies us from all things from which we could not be justified by the law of Moses." Nothing unclean or defiled can enter heaven. This is God's own testimony: "There shall in no wise enter into it anything that defileth, neither whatsoever worketh abomination, or maketh a lie, but they which are written in the Lamb's book of life," (see Revelation 21.27). How clearly do we see from this testimony who shall not and who shall enter the holy Jerusalem, that heavenly city which the glory of God lightens, and of which the Lamb is the everlasting light. No defiled persons can enter there-in; and none but those whose names are written in the Lamb's book of life; for these He has "washed from their sins in His own blood, and made them kings and priests unto God and His Father," see Revelation 1. 5-6). Therefore they are "without fault before the throne of God," (see Revelation 14. 5).

But besides this their title, there must be also a meetness for this heavenly city, according to the words of the apostle: "Giving thanks unto the Father, which hath made us meet to be partakers of the inheritance of the saints in light," (see Colossians 1. 12). Whilst here below, then, we must learn to sing some notes of that joyous anthem, which will issue in full, uninterrupted harmony from the hearts and lips of the redeemed in the realms above, when that glorious company will ever cry, "Alleluia; Salvation, and glory, and honour, and power unto the LORD our God." O what a voice will that be, "the voice of a great multitude, and as the voice of many waters and as the voice of mighty thunderings, saying, Alleluia: for the Lord God omnipotent reigneth. Let us be glad and rejoice, and give honour to Him: for the marriage of the Lamb to come, and his wife hath made herself ready," (see Revelation 19.1, 6-7). If then we are to sit down among those blessed ones who are called unto the marriage supper of the Lamb, not only must we be "arrayed in fine linen, clean and white, for the fine linen is the righteousness of the saints" (see Revelation 19. 8-9) but we must have had the "kingdom of God, which is righteousness and peace and joy in the Holy Ghost" (see Romans 14. 17) set up in our hearts. This, then, is what I mean when I speak of a religion which will take us to heaven. It consists, as I have said, in two things, 1. a title to heaven; 2. a meetness for heaven. Without a title we could not possess it; without a meetness we could not enjoy it. The one is from the work of the Son of God in His flesh; the other from the work of God the Holy Ghost on our heart.

But now view the subject in a somewhat different light, and yet still bearing upon the same grand truth. At the close of what is called "The Sermon on the Mount," the Lord describes two different characters. The one he likens to a wise man who built his house upon a rock, and the other to a foolish man who built his house upon the sand. The man who built upon a rock built for eternity; so that when "the rain descended, and the floods came and the winds blew and beat upon that house," it fell not. And why? For this simple reason; "It was founded upon a rock." But how different was the case of the foolish man, who built his house upon the sand, upon the quicksand of human merit. When "the rain descended, and the floods came, and the winds blew, and beat upon that house, it fell, and great was the fall of it." The two houses, as long as the weather was fine and fair, might look equally well, and seem to stand equally strong; but the storm tried each by trying the foundation on which each was built. In that storm the one stood as firm as adamant; the other fell into a shapeless ruin, of which the very fragments were swept away by the rushing floods. See then to the foundation of your house; whether you are building upon Christ or upon self; are founding your hopes upon the rock, or are rearing them upon the sand.

THE REDEEMED IN HEAVEN[32]

Revelation 7. 9-17

"After this I beheld, and, lo, a great multitude, which no man could number, of all nations, and kindreds, and people, and tongues, stood before the throne, and before the Lamb, clothed with white robes, and palms in their hands." I have been a reader, and, I may say, a student of the Scriptures for thirty-four or thirty-five years, and I hope the Lord has given me some entrance by faith into the meaning of His holy Word. But there are parts of the Scriptures which to me are very dark, and of which I have not, as I feel, any real knowledge. Such is the Book of Revelation. No part of Scripture has more perplexed me to understand its meaning than this holy book. And yet there is a promise: *"Blessed is he that readeth, and they that hear the words of this prophecy, and keep those things which are written therein"* (see Revelation 1. 3).

But though much of the Revelation is so dark and mysterious, yet there are blessed portions of it which are full of sweet experimental instruction; and such is the passage before us, where John *"beheld, and, lo, a great multitude, which no man could number, of all nations, and kindreds, and people, and tongues, stood before the throne, and before the Lamb, clothed with white robes, and palms in their hands."* These seem to signify the elect church of God, the whole assembly of the redeemed; for John views them in their glorious church state at the second coming of the Son of God, when all the saints will come with Him and will form a great multitude which no man can number.

Now John saw them stand before the throne, and they were collected of all nations, and kindreds, and people, and tongues; to show the universality of the gospel, and how the Lord chooses of every nation where the gospel is powerfully preached as a seed to serve Him. They stood before the throne of God and before the Lamb who sat upon the throne. And how did they stand? *"Clothed with white robes";* which signifies that they stand before God without spot or wrinkle or any such thing, as being washed in the atoning blood of the Lord the Lamb, and thus free from blemish in the eyes of Him who is of infinite purity. And they bore *"palms in their hands";* which were marks that they had fought the good fight, had overcome, and had achieved the victory; in memory of which the palm, which was borne by the ancient victors, was put into their hands, that they might bear it before the throne and wave it triumphantly over their heads.

And John heard them cry *"with a loud voice, saying, Salvation to our God which sitteth upon the throne, and unto the Lamb";* ascribing all the praise and glory of their salvation to God who sat upon the throne; tracing it all up unto the eternal purposes and electing love of God the Father, and to the atoning blood and dying love of God the Son. And they all joined in one universal chorus. There was no discordant note among them. They all as with one united voice cried aloud and ascribed salvation for ever and ever, with all its blessings, as belonging to our God that sitteth upon the throne, and unto His dear Son.

"And all the angels stood round about the throne, and about the elders and the four beasts, and fell before the throne on their faces, and worshipped God." This throne of God was surrounded by thousands and tens of thousands of bright and holy angels. Now you will observe that first there is the throne on which God sits; then there is the Lamb who sits with Him on the throne; then there are the elders that represent the churches; and lastly the four disciples or living creatures which represent the ministers; and these all stand before and close to the throne. Then in a circle round about it stand the holy angels as witnesses of the triumphs of the cross of Christ—as joining, not in the song of redeeming love, for they were not redeemed, but still, with holy approbation they unite in praising and blessing Jesus, the Lord God Almighty; for they are represented as falling before the throne on their faces, with all humility and prostration of mind, and worshipping God in union with the church.

And what do they say in this holy song? They give to God a seven-fold blessing: *"Blessing, and glory, and wisdom, and thanksgiving, and honour, and power, and might, be unto our God for ever and ever. Amen."* They said *"Amen,"* assenting to God's purposes, yielding a solemn "So be it" to the work of redeeming love, and ascribing to God all the blessings of salvation, and the sense of their own standing, and all the glory of the scheme of salvation, and all the wisdom which prompted the Almighty to devise it; and thanksgiving, as being the subject of eternal praise; and honour, as justly belonging to Him from whom it came; and power, whereby He accomplished it all; and might, whereby He gained the victory. This seven-fold blessing they ascribed to God. And then, with loud acclaim, they added, "So be it."

"And one of the elders answered, saying unto me, What are these which are arrayed in white robes? and whence came they?" This question was put, not as though the elder did not know it, for he was going to give the answer, but to call John's attention more especially to it. But John did not know it. Therefore he said, *"Sir, thou knowest. Tell me."* Then comes the answer from the mouth of the elder who speaks in the name of the church: *"And he said to me, These are they which came out of great tribulation, and have washed their robes, and made them white in the blood of the Lamb."* They came out of great tribulation: it is *"through much tribulation"* we are to enter the kingdom. They were in it and came out of it through the power and might of God displayed in them; but this was not their title to eternal bliss. Not all their sufferings nor sorrows gave them any power to inherit glory. This was their title, that they had *"washed their robes and made them while in the blood of the Lamb."* They disclaimed all goodness of their own. They had a view of the fountain of Christ's blood; they descended into that fountain as Naaman descended into the River Jordan; and in that fountain they washed away all their sins, as Naaman washed away his leprosy in Jordan's waters. They *"washed their robes and made them white in the blood of the Lamb."*

"Therefore are they before the throne of God, and serve Him day and night in His temple." Why are they before the throne of God? Because they have *"washed their robes and made them white in the blood of the Lamb."* Whom do they serve? God. Where do they serve Him? In His temple. How long do they serve Him? Day and night; because being sanctified spirits, having immortal souls and

immortal bodies, they are able to render Him unceasing service. *"And He that sitteth on the throne shall dwell among them."*
"They shall hunger no more, neither thirst any more; neither shall the sun light on them, nor any heat." To the sun of temptation or the heat of God's anger they shall not be exposed any more.

"For the Lamb which is in the midst of the throne shall feed them" with manifestations of His Person; *"and shall lead them unto living fountains of waters"*—that is, the rivers of pleasure which are at God's right hand for evermore; *"and God Himself"*—their God and Father— *"shall wipe away all tears from their eyes."*

O what a glorious company! O what a mercy it will be if we, in this vale of tears, should ever reach that heavenly shore, stand before that throne in robes washed white in the blood of the Lamb, and join in singing that immortal song which saints and angels will sing in sweet unison!

Give me the wings of faith to rise
Within the veil and see
The saints above, how great their joys,
How bright their glories be.

Once they were mourning here below,
And wet their couch with tears;
They wrestled hard, as we do now,
With sins, and doubts, and fears.

I ask them whence their victory came,
They with united breath,
Ascribe their conquest to the Lamb,
Their triumph to His death.

They marked the footsteps that He trod,
(His zeal inspired their breast);
And following their incarnate God,
Possess the promised rest.

Our glorious Leader claims our praise
For His own pattern given;
While the long cloud of witnesses
Shows the same path to heaven.

THE LORD JESUS CHRIST AS THE SON OF MAN[33]

—

"Fear not; I am the first and the last:" Revelation 1. 18.

—

I do not know a more solemn or weighty part of the Word of God than the messages which our gracious Lord sent by the hand of John to the seven churches in Asia, which we find contained in chapters 2 and 3 of the Book of Revelation. As introductory to these messages, and to give them greater weight and power, as well as to furnish a general introduction to the whole of the book, our adorable Lord appeared to John in a very conspicuous and glorious revelation, of which we have the record in the first chapter. He tells us there that he "was in the isle of Patmos for the Word of God and for the testimony of Jesus Christ." Being, thus, the Lord's prisoner, he "was in the Spirit on the Lord's day, and heard behind him a great voice as of a trumpet, saying, I am Alpha and Omega, the first and the last."

1. If you carefully examine the distinctive features of this revelation, you will not see in it His *priestly* character. He did not appear to John as the High Priest over the house of God; as the Mediator at the right hand of the Father; as the Intercessor able to save to the uttermost all who come unto God by Him. But He appeared as King in Zion in all the dignity of regal majesty. You will easily see this from casting your eye upon the description which John gives of His glorious Person. Thus, he says that "His head and His hairs were white like wool, as white as snow." This feature symbolises His eternity; for you will recollect that "the Ancient of Days," who from the context is evidently the Father, is represented in Daniel 7. 9 with "the hair of His head like the pure wool." But why should this symbolise eternal duration? It is because grey hair represents age in man; and thus in type and figure His hairs being white like wool, as white as snow, represent duration, that is, eternal duration in the Son of God. He is called, in Isaiah 9. 6, "the everlasting Father," or as Bishop Lowth renders it, "the Father of the everlasting age;" and His "goings forth" are declared by the prophet Micah to have been "from of old, from everlasting." Now, it is to Him in His regal character that this description applies. The prophet Isaiah, therefore, says in connection with His being "the everlasting Father," that He is "the Prince of Peace;" and that "of the increase of

86

His government and peace there shall be no end;" and the prophet Micah, in the passage which I have quoted, declares that He is "ruler in Israel."

2. Another feature observable in this description is, that *"His eyes were as a flame of fire,"* not tender, gracious and sympathising, as would have been the eyes of the high priest; but the eyes of a King in His regal majesty, flashing forth rays and beams to illuminate and gladden those who believe, and to smite down, as with so many lightning shafts, those who live and die in their unbelief; searching all hearts and trying all reins, and like flames of fire penetrating into the depths of every human breast.

3. Another striking feature in this description is that *"His feet were like unto fine brass"*—not torn or bearing any marks upon them of the cruel nails whereby He was fastened to the cross, but bright, shining and glorious as become the feet of an enthroned King, able to dispense the riches of His grace, and yet swift to move forward on errands of vengeance.

4. Another noticeable feature was His *voice*, which was *"as the sound of many waters;"* so full was it, melodious, powerful and falling upon the ear like water rushing from a height. You have sat at times, it may be, near a waterfall, and you have heard the rush of the waters as they fell down the steep rock. What strength, and yet what harmonious melody, were blended together in the sound. What a calm stole over your mind, and how, as you breathed the air around you, so cool and fresh, a spirit of meditation came over you as your ears listened to the noise of the ever-falling waters in their ceaseless melody! Thus, in it there were combined these three things: power, continuance and melody. And are not these three things characteristic of the voice of Christ as "the voice of the Lord upon many waters" spoken of by the Psalmist?

1. It is *powerful;* for "with the word of a king there is power;" and it is expressly said of it, "The voice of the Lord is powerful, the voice of the Lord is full of majesty."

2. It is *continuous,* for this voice is ever speaking to the hearts of His people.

3. And we need not tell those who have heard it that it is most melodious, for every accent is full of sweetness; as the Bride said in

her description of her Beloved, "His mouth is most sweet." (See Song of Solomon 5. 16).

4. Another characteristic feature of this glorious Person is that He "had in His *right hand seven stars.*" These He himself explains as being the angels, that is, the presiding ministers or pastors of the seven churches. They are called "stars" as shining in the Christian firmament with conspicuous lustre, as giving light to the churches, directing them to Christ, and pointing out the way of salvation, as stars were used for guides in ancient navigation, and also to rule the churches, as stars rule the night. As held also in Christ's hand, it shows how that they are wholly at His disposal, held up only by His mighty power, preserved from error and apostasy only by His grace, and used as instruments to do His work and shine in His light.

5. Another conspicuous feature, which I may name, is *His sword. "And out of His mouth went a sharp two-edged sword."* This signifies the Word which He speaks with a divine power, for it corresponds with the description given of the Word of God by the apostle, "For the Word of God is quick, and powerful, and sharper than any two-edged sword, piercing even to the dividing asunder of soul and spirit, and of the joints and marrow, and is a discerner of the thoughts and intents of the heart." (See Hebrews 4. 12). By this sword He searches the heart, as He says: "All the churches shall know that I am He which searcheth the reins and hearts" (See Revelation 2. 23); and by this sword he fights also against all evil doers, as He declares, "Repent; or else I will come unto thee quickly, and will fight against thee with the sword of My mouth." (See Revelation 2. 16). This sword carries with it death when it is lifted up against the impenitent and unbelieving: "And I will kill her children with death." (See Revelation 2. 23).

6. The last feature which I shall mention is the glory of His countenance. *"And His countenance was as the sun shineth in his strength."* This is a representation of His glory as the Sun of Righteousness; and as such He appeared to the three favoured disciples when He was transfigured before them, for "His face did shine as the sun." (See Matthew 17. 2).

Now this wonderful description of the glory of the Son of God, as seen by John, was to prepare him for the reception of the

Revelation with which he was to be favoured for the benefit of the church in all time, and especially to give weight, authority and power to the messages sent by him to the seven churches.

In these messages to the seven churches, there are certain features which are common to all, and there are certain features which are distinctive of each.

Of the features common to all the messages, there are chiefly three.

1. The first is, *"I know thy works."* How accordant these words are with the description of His eyes as a flame of fire; and how they show us that every word and work, every thought and imagination of our hearts are naked and open before the eyes of Him with whom we have to do. We may deceive ourselves, but we cannot deceive Him. He knows all that we are and have been, and is perfectly acquainted with everything in us both in nature and grace. It is good when a feeling sense of this makes us watch our words and works, and to desire that they might be pleasing in His sight, and that what we do in His name might have His approbation in our hearts and consciences.

2. Another common feature, and one that generally winds up the message (as, "I know thy works," introduces it), is, "He that hath an ear, let him hear what the Spirit saith unto the churches." These words extend the message beyond the church to which they were spoken, and address themselves to every one to whom the Word comes, and to whom an ear is given to hear and receive it. Thus each message sent to the churches becomes a message sent personally to us. If we have a spiritually circumcised ear, if we are willing to listen to the voice of the Lord, He speaks to us in every message as personally and as distinctly as He spoke to each individual church. It is indeed an unspeakable blessing to have this ear given to us that we may receive in humility, simplicity and godly sincerity what the Lord speaks in the Word of his grace. It is by His Word that He knocks at the door of our hearts; and what a blessing He has pronounced on the man who hears His voice and opens the door when he hears the knock, like a fond and affectionate wife when she hears the knock of her husband at the door of his house: "Behold, I stand at the door, and knock: if any man hear My voice, and open the door, I will come

in to him, and will sup with him, and he with Me." (See Revelation 3. 20).

    3.The last common feature which I shall name, is the promise given *"to him that overcometh,"* varied in every message with a special promise attached to it.

Join all the glorious names
Of wisdom, love, and power,
That ever mortals knew,
That angels ever bore;
All are too mean to speak H-is worth,
Too mean to set my Saviour forth.

But O what gentle terms
What condescending ways,
Does our Redeemer use
To teach His heavenly grace!
My eyes with joy and wonder see
What forms of love He bears for me.

Arrayed in mortal flesh,
He like an angel stands,
And holds the promises
And pardons in His hands;
Commissioned from His Father's throne,
To make His grace to mortals known.

Jesus, my great High Priest,
Offered His blood and died;
My guilty conscience seeks
No sacrifice beside.
His powerful blood did once atone,
And now it pleads before the throne.

My Advocate appears
For my defence on high;
The Father bows His ears,
And lays His thunder by.
Not all that hell or sin can say,
Shall turn His heart, His love away.

My dear, almighty Lord,
My Conqueror and my King,
Thy sceptre and Thy sword,
Thy reigning grace I sing;
Thine is the power; behold, I sit,
In willing bonds, beneath Thy feet.

BIBLIOGRAPHY

Most of the extracts are taken from sermons reported on the following occasions:

1. Gower Street Chapel, London – Lord's Day morning 21st July 1867

2. Zoar Chapel, Great Alie Street, London – Lord's Day morning 16th August 1846

3. Gower Street Chapel, London – Lord's Day evening 27th July 1856

4. North Street Chapel, Stamford – Lord's Day morning 6th March 1859

5. Eden Street Chapel, Hampstead, London – Tuesday evening 27th July 1847

6. Providence Chapel, Eden Street, London – 28th July 1850

7. Providence Chapel, Eden Street, London – Lord's Day morning 20th August 1843

8. *Gospel Standard* – October 1891 page 411

9. Zoar Chapel, Great Alie Street, London – Evening 8th July 1841

10. Artillery Street Chapel, Bishopsgate, London – Wednesday evening 23rd June 1841

11. Eden Street Chapel, Hampstead, London – Lord's Day evening 24th August 1845

12. Zoar Chapel, Great Alie Street, London – Thursday evening 18th July 1861

13. Salem, Landport, Portsmouth – Thursday evening 2nd August 1853

14. Eden Street Chapel, Hampstead, London – 2nd August 1853

15. Gower Street Chapel, London – Lord's Day evening 21st May 1865

16. Allington, Near Devizes – Lord's Day afternoon 19th September 1841

17. Zoar Chapel, Great Alie Street, London – Lord's Day morning 13th July 1845

18. Zoar Chapel, Great Alie Street, London – Lord's Day evening 3rd August 1845

19. Providence Chapel, Oakham – Lord's Day afternoon 11th June 1865

20. Woodbridge Chapel, Clerkenwell, London – Lord's Day morning 14th May 1865

21. Providence Chapel, Oakham – 2nd February 1847

22. Providence Chapel, Oakham – Tuesday evening 4th October 1864

23. Gower Street Chapel, London – Lord's Day morning 19th July 1868

24. North Street Chapel, Stamford – Lord's Day morning 31st January 1864

25. Providence Chapel, Oakham – 8th June 1845

26. Eden Street Chapel, Hampstead, London – Tuesday evening 27th July 1847

27. Park Street Chapel, Nottingham – Thursday evening 23rd September 1858

28. North Street Chapel, Stamford – 13th December 1857

29. Park Street Chapel, Nottingham – Thursday evening 23rd September 1858

30. Providence Chapel, Oakham – Lord's Day morning 22nd June 1845

31. *Ears From Harvested Sheaves* – page 30

32. Lord's Day morning – 8th December 1861 – *Gospel Standard* 1986 page 139

33. Gower Street Chapel, London – Lord's Day morning 21st June 1868

OTHER BOOKS AVAILABLE

Through Baca's Vale: J.C.Philpot
Daily readings
Ears From Harvested Sheaves: : J.C.Philpot
Daily readings
J.C.Philpot Sermons
168 sermons in 12 volumes
William Tiptaft: by J.C.Philpot
Biography of this eminent preacher
The Seceders: by J.H. Philpot
The story of J.C. Philpot and William Tiptaft.
"Manna"
A book of sermons by J.C.Philpot
Sin and Salvation: by J.C. Philpot
Two sides to real religion.
The King's Daughters: by B.A.Ramsbottom
The lives of 16 Godly women
In Search of Freedom: by J.R.Broome
The story of the Pilgrim Fathers
Bible Doctrines Simply Explained: by B.A. Ramsbottom
A simple presentation of Christian doctrine.
The Old is Better: by A.J. Levell
Some Bible versions considered
Spirit of Truth: by J.R. Broome
Some aspects of charismatic teaching.
Christmas Evans: by B.A. Ramsbottom
Welsh evangelist of 18th century.
Christian Marriage and Divorce: by L.S.B. Hyde
Marriage and divorce in the light of scripture teaching.
Cremation: by A.J. Levell
Not for Christians.
Miracles of Jesus (series of 7): by B.A. Ramsbottom
Simply retold and illustrated for young children.
Stranger Than Fiction: by B.A. Ramsbottom
The Life of William Kiffin.
Reformation and Counter Reformation: by J.R. Broome
Attempts to change the Protestant constitution.
John Knox: by J.R. Broome
16th Century Scottish reformer.

Servant of a Covenant God: by J.R. Broome
Life and times of John Warburton.
More Than Notion: by J.H. Alexander
Spiritual experiences of a remarkable group of people.
Creation: by John Barker
The Bible consistent with true science.
John Gill: by J.R. Broome
18th Century theologian.
In All Their Affliction: by Murdoch Campbell
Words of comfort for Christians.
Unanswered Prayer: by G.D. Buss
The difficulty of seemingly unanswered prayer.
Gadsby's Hymns
A selection of hymns compiled by William Gadsby.
To Glory in a Blaze: by J.R. Broome
The 16th century English martyrs.
Six Remarkable Ministers: by B.A. Ramsbottom
How God made them to be ministers of the gospel.
Divine Guidance: by B.A. Ramsbottom
How may I know God's will?
John Kershaw
Pastor for 50 years in Rochdale.
Why Denominations?: by J.A. Watts
The dangers of modern ecumenism examined.
Valiant for Truth: by J.H.Gosden
Life and letters of J.K.Popham
Mary Jones and Her Bible: by Mary Ropes
How a Welsh girl obtained a Bible
Bible Lessons for Little Ones: by Gary TenBroeke
An aid for parents and Sunday School Teachers
Bibles
The Word of God. A selection of the Authorised Version.

For a full list of publications please write to:

Gospel Standard Trust Publications
12(b) Roundwood Lane
Harpenden, Hertfordshire
AL5 3DD, England